The Reasoned Sch

The Reasoned Schemer

Second Edition

Daniel P. Friedman
William E. Byrd
Oleg Kiselyov
Jason Hemann

Drawings by Duane Bibby

Foreword by Guy Lewis Steele Jr. and Gerald Jay Sussman
Afterword by Robert A. Kowalski

The MIT Press
Cambridge, Massachusetts
London, England

This book was set in Computer Modern by the authors using LaTeX. Printed and bound in the United States of America.

Library of Congress Cataloging-in-Publication Data

Names: Friedman, Daniel P., author.
Title: The reasoned schemer / Daniel P. Friedman, William E. Byrd, Oleg Kiselyov, and Jason Hemann ; drawings by Duane Bibby ; foreword by Guy Lewis Steele Jr. and Gerald Jay Sussman ; afterword by Robert A. Kowalski.
Description: Second edition. — Cambridge, MA : The MIT Press, [2018] — Includes index.
Identifiers: LCCN 2017046328 — ISBN 9780262535519 (pbk. : alk. paper)
Subjects: LCSH: Scheme (Computer program language)
Classification: LCC QA76.73.S34 F76 2018 — DDC 005.13/3–dc23 LC record available at https://lccn.loc.gov/2017046328

10 9 8 7 6 5 4 3 2

To Mary, Sara, Rachel, Shannon and Rob,
and to the memory of Brian.

To Mom & Dad, Brian & Claudia, Mary & Donald, and Renzhong & Lea.

To Dad.

To Mom and Dad.

((**Contents**)

Foreword

In Plato's great dialogue *Meno*, written about 2400 years ago, we are treated to a wonderful teaching demonstration. Socrates demonstrates to Meno that it is possible to teach a deep truth of plane geometry to a relatively uneducated boy (who knows simple arithmetic but only a little of geometry) by asking a carefully planned sequence of leading questions. Socrates first shows Meno that the boy certainly has some incorrect beliefs, both about geometry and about what he does or does not know: although the boy thinks he can construct a square with double the area of a given square, he doesn't even know that his idea is wrong. Socrates leads the boy to understand that his proposed construction does not work, then remarks to Meno, "Mark now the farther development. I shall only ask him, and not teach him, and he shall share the enquiry with me: and do you watch and see if you find me telling or explaining anything to him, instead of eliciting his opinion." By a deliberate and very detailed line of questioning, Socrates leads the boy to confirm the steps of a correct construction. Socrates concludes that the boy really knew the correct result all along—that the knowledge was innate.

Nowadays we know (from the theory of NP-hard problems, for example) that it can be substantially harder to find the solution to a problem than to confirm a proposed solution. Unlike Socrates himself, we regard "Socratic dialogue" as a form of teaching, one that is actually quite difficult to do well.

For over four decades, since his book *The Little LISPer* appeared in 1974, Dan Friedman, working with many friends and students, has used superbly constructed Socratic dialogue to teach deep truths about programming by asking carefully planned sequences of leading questions. They take the reader on a journey that is entertaining as well as educational; as usual, the examples are mostly about food. While working through this book, we each began to feel that we already knew the results innately. "I see—I knew this all along! How could it be otherwise?" Perhaps Socrates was right after all?

Earlier books from Dan and company taught the essentials of recursion and functional programming. *The Reasoned Schemer* goes deeper, taking a gentle path to mastery of the essentials of relational programming by building on a base of functional programming. By the end of the book, we are able to use relational methods effectively; but even better, we learn how to erect an elegant relational language on the functional substrate. It was not obvious up front that this could be done in a manner so accessible and pretty—but step by step we can easily confirm the presented solution.

☞ You know, don't you, that *The Little Schemer*, like *The Little LISPer*, was a fun read?

☞ And is it not true that you like to read about food and about programming?

☞ And is not the book in your hands exactly that sort of book, the kind you would like to read?

Guy Lewis Steele Jr. and Gerald Jay Sussman
Cambridge, Massachusetts
August 2017

Preface

The Reasoned Schemer explores the often bizarre, sometimes frustrating, and always fascinating world of relational programming.

The first book in the "little" series, *The Little Schemer*, presents ideas from functional programming: each program corresponds to a mathematical function. A simple example of a function is *square*, which multiplies an integer by itself: $square(4) = 16$, and so forth. In contrast, *The Reasoned Schemer* presents ideas from relational programming, where programs correspond to relations that generalize mathematical functions. For example, the relation $square^o$ generalizes *square* by relating pairs of integers: $square^o(4, 16)$ relates 4 with 16, and so forth. We call a relation supplied with arguments, such as $square^o(4, 16)$, a *goal*. A goal can *succeed*, *fail*, or *have no value.*

The great advantage of $square^o$ over *square* is its flexibility. By passing a *variable* representing an unknown value—rather than a concrete integer—to $square^o$, we can express a variety of problems involving integers and their squares. For example, the goal $square^o(3, x)$ succeeds by associating 9 with the variable x. The goal $square^o(y, 9)$ succeeds twice, by separately associating -3 and then 3 with y. If we have written our $square^o$ relation properly, the goal $square^o(z, 5)$ fails, and we conclude that there is no integer whose square is 5; otherwise, the goal has no value, and we cannot draw any conclusions about z. Using two variables lets us create a goal $square^o(w, v)$ that succeeds *an unbounded number* of times, enumerating all pairs of integers such that the second integer is the square of the first. Used together, the goals $square^o(x, y)$ and $square^o(-3, x)$ succeed—regardless of the ordering of the goals—associating 9 with x and 81 with y. Welcome to the strange and wonderful world of relational programming!

This book has three themes: how to understand, use, and create relations and goals (chapters 1–8); when to use *non-relational* operators that take us from relational programming to its impure variant (chapter 9); and how to implement a complete relational programming language on top of Scheme (chapter 10 and appendix A).

We show how to translate Scheme functions from most of the chapters of *The Little Schemer* into relations. Once the power of programming with relations is understood, we then exploit this power by defining in chapters 7 and 8 familiar arithmetic operators as relations. The $+^o$ relation can not only add but also subtract; $*^o$ can not only multiply but also factor numbers; and log^o can not only find the logarithm given a number and a base but also find the base given a logarithm and a number. Just as we can define the subtraction relation from the addition relation, we can define the exponentiation relation from the logarithm relation. In general, given ($*^o$ x y z) we can specify what we know about these numbers (their values, whether they are odd or even, etc.) and ask $*^o$ to find the unspecified values. We don't specify *how* to accomplish the task; rather, we describe *what* we want in the result.

This relational thinking is yet another way of understanding computation and it can be expressed using a tiny low-level language. We use this language to introduce the fundamental notions of relational programming in chapter 1, and as the foundation of our implementation in chapter 10. Later in chapter 1 we switch to a slightly friendlier syntax—inspired by Scheme's *equal?*, **let**, **cond**, and **define**—allowing us to more easily translate Scheme functions into relations. Here is the higher-level syntax:

($\equiv$ t_0 t_1) (**fresh** (x ...) g ...) (**cond**^{e} (g ...) ...) (**defrel** (*name* x ...) g ...)

The function $\equiv$ is defined in chapter 10; **fresh**, **cond**^{e}, and **defrel** are defined in the appendix **Connecting the Wires** using Scheme's syntactic extension mechanism.

The only requirement for understanding relational programming is familiarity with lists and recursion. The implementation in chapter 10 requires an understanding of functions as values. That is, a function can be both an argument to and the value of a function call. And that's it—we assume no further knowledge of mathematics or logic.

We have taken certain liberties with punctuation to increase clarity. Specifically, we have omitted question marks in the left-hand side of frames that end with a special symbol or a closing right parenthesis. We have done this, for example, to avoid confusion with function names that end with a question mark, and to reduce clutter around the parentheses of lists.

Food appears in examples throughout the book for two reasons. First, food is easier to visualize than abstract symbols; we hope the food imagery helps you to better understand the examples and concepts. Second, we want to provide a little distraction. We know how frustrating the subject matter can be, thus these culinary diversions are for whetting your appetite. As such, we hope that thinking about food will cause you to stop reading and have a bite.

You are now ready to start. Good luck! We hope you enjoy the book.

Bon appétit!

Daniel P. Friedman
Bloomington, Indiana

William E. Byrd
Salt Lake City, Utah

Oleg Kiselyov
Sendai, Japan

Jason Hemann
Bloomington, Indiana

Acknowledgements

We thank Guy Steele and Gerry Sussman, the creators of Scheme, for contributing the foreword, and Bob Kowalski, one of the creators of logic programming, for contributing the afterword. We are grateful for their pioneering work that laid the foundations for the ideas in this book.

Mitch Wand has been an indispensable sounding board for both editions. Duane Bibby, whose artwork sets the tone for these "Little" books, has provided several new illustrations. Ron Garcia, David Christiansen, and Shriram Krishnamurthi and Malavika Jayaram kindly suggested the delicious courses for the banquet in chapter 10. Carl Eastlund and David Christiansen graciously shared their type-setting macros with us. Jon Loldrup inspired us to completely revise the first chapter. Michael Ballantyne, Nada Amin, Lisa Zhang, Nick Drozd, and Oliver Bračevac offered insightful observations. Greg Rosenblatt gave us detailed comments on every chapter in the final draft of the book. Amr Sabry and the Computer Science Department's administrative staff at Indiana University's School of Informatics, Computing, and Engineering have made being here a true pleasure. The teaching staff and students of Indiana University's C311 and B521 courses are always an inspiration. C311 student Jeremy Penery discovered and fixed an error in the definition of log^o from the first edition. Finally, we have received great leadership from the staff at MIT Press, specifically Christine Savage and our editor, Marie Lee. We offer our grateful appreciation and thanks to all.

Will thanks Matt and Cristina Might, and the entire Might family, for their support. He also thanks the members of the U Combinator research group at the University of Utah, and gratefully acknowledges the support of DARPA under agreement number AFRL FA8750-15-2-0092.

Acknowledgements from the First Edition

This book would not have been possible without earlier work on implementing and using logic systems with Matthias Felleisen, Anurag Mendhekar, Jon Rossie, Michael Levin, Steve Ganz, and Venkatesh Choppella. Steve showed how to partition Prolog's named relations into unnamed functions, while Venkatesh helped characterize the types in this early logic system. We thank them for their effort during this developmental stage.

There are many others we wish to thank. Mitch Wand struggled through an early draft and spent several days in Bloomington clarifying the semantics of the language, which led to the elimination of superfluous language forms. We also appreciate Kent Dybvig's and Yevgeniy Makarov's comments on the first few chapters of an early draft and Amr Sabry's Haskell implementation of the language.

We gratefully acknowledge Abdulaziz Ghuloum's insistence that we remove some abstract material from the introductory chapter. In addition, Aziz's suggestions significantly clarified the **run** interface. Also incredibly helpful were the detailed criticisms of Chung-chieh Shan, Erik Hilsdale, John Small, Ronald Garcia, Phill Wolf, and Jos Koot. We are especially grateful to Chung-chieh for **Connecting the Wires** so masterfully in the final implementation.

We thank David Mack and Kyle Blocher for teaching this material to students in our undergraduate programming languages course and for making observations that led to many improvements to this book. We also thank those students who not only learned from the material but helped us to clarify its presentation.

There are several people we wish to thank for contributions not directly related to the ideas in the book. We would be remiss if we did not acknowledge Dorai Sitaram's incredibly clever Scheme typesetting program, SLaTeX. We are grateful for Matthias Felleisen's typesetting macros (created for *The Little Schemer*), and for Oscar Waddell's implementation of a tool that selectively expands Scheme macros. Also, we thank Shriram Krishnamurthi for reminding us of a promise we made that the food would be vegetarian in the next *little* book. Finally, we thank Bob Prior, our editor, for his encouragement and enthusiasm for this effort.

Since the First Edition

Over a dozen years have passed since the first edition and much has changed.

There are five categories of changes since the first edition. These categories include changes to the language, changes to the implementation, changes to the **Laws** and **Commandments**, along with the introduction of the **Translation**, changes to the prose, and changes to how we express quasiquoted lists.

There are seven changes to the language. First, we have generalized the behavior of **cond**^{e}, **fresh**, and **run***, which has allowed us to simplify the language by removing three forms: **cond**^{i}, **all**, and **all**^{i}. Second, we have introduced a new form, **defrel**, which defines relations, and which replaces uses of **define**. Use of **defrel** is not strictly necessary—see the workaround as part of the footnote in frame 82 of chapter 1 and in frame 61 of chapter 10. Third, $\equiv$ now calls a version of *unify* that uses *occurs?* prior to extending a substitution. Fourth, we made changes to the **run*** interface. **run*** can now take a single identifier, as in (**run*** x ($\equiv$ 5 x)), which is cleaner than the notation in the first edition. We have also extended **run*** to take a list of one or more identifiers, as in (**run*** (x y z) ($\equiv$ x y)). These identifiers are bound to unique fresh variables, and the reified value of these variables is returned in a list. These changes apply as well to **run**^{n}, which is now written as **run** n. Fifth, we have dropped the **else** keyword from **cond**^{e}, **cond**^{a}, and **cond**^{u}, making every line in these forms have the same structure. Sixth, the operators, *always*^{o} and *never*^{o} have become relations of zero arguments, rather than goals. Last, in chapter 1 we have introduced the low-level binary disjunction ($disj_2$) and conjuction ($conj_2$), but only as a way to explain **cond**^{e} and **fresh**.

The implementation is fully described in chapter 10. Though in the early part of this chapter we still explain variables, substitutions, and other concepts related to unification. We then explain streams, including suspensions, $disj_2$, and $conj_2$. We show how *append*^{o} (introduced in chapter 4, swapped with what was formerly chapter 5) macro-expands to a relation in the lower-level language introduced in chapter 1. Last, we show how to write *ifte* (for **cond**^{a}) and *once* (for **cond**^{u}).

We define in chapter 10 as much of the implementation as possible as Scheme *functions.* This allows us to greatly simplify the Scheme *macros* in appendix A that define the syntax of our relational language. To further simplify the implementation, appendix A defines two recursive help macros: **disj**, built from #u and $disj_2$; and **conj**, built from #s and $conj_2$. The appendix then defines the seven user-level macros, of which only **fresh** and **cond**^{a} are recursive. We have also added a short guide on understanding our style of writing macros. In the absence of macros, the functions in chapter 10 can be defined in any language that supports functions as values.

Next, we have clarified the **Laws** and **Commandments**. In addition to these improvements, we have added explicit **Translation** rules. For example, we now demand that, in any function we transform into a relation, every last **cond** line begins with #t instead of **else**. This makes the **Laws** and **Commandments** more uniform and easier to internalize. In addition, this simple change improves understanding of the newly-added **Translation**, and makes it easier to distinguish those Scheme functions that use #t from those in the implementation chapter that use **else**.

We have made many changes to the prose of the book. We have completely rewritten chapter 1. There we introduce the notion of *fusing* two variables, meaning a reference to one is the same as a reference to the other. Chapters 2–5 have been re-ordered and restructured, with some examples dropped and others added. In these four chapters we explain and exploit the **Translation**, so that transforming a function, written with our aforementioned changes to **cond**'s **else**, is more direct. We have shortened chapter 6, which now focuses exclusively on $always^o$ and $never^o$. Chapter 7 is mostly the same, with a few minor, yet important, modifications. Chapter 8 is also mostly the same, but here we have added a detailed description of $split^o$. Understanding $split^o$ is necessary for understanding $\div^o$ and log^o, and we have re-organized some of the complicated relations so that they can be read more easily. Chapter 9, swapped with what was formerly chapter 10, is mostly the same. The first half places more emphasis on necessary restrictions by using new **Laws** and **Commandments** for **cond**^{a} and **cond**^{u}. The second half is mostly unchanged, but restricts the relations to be first-order, to mirror the rest of the book. We, however, finish by shifting to a higher-order relation, allowing the same relation $enumerate^o$ to enumerate $+^o$, $*^o$, and exp^o, and we describe how the remaining relations, $\div^o$ and log^o, can also be enumerated.

Finally, we have replaced implicit punctuation of quasiquoted expressions with explicit punctuation (backtick and comma).

The Reasoned Schemer

1.
Playthings

Welcome back.

1 It is good to be here, again.

Have you finished *The Little Schemer*?[†]

2 #f.

[†] Or *The Little LISPer*.

That's okay.

Do you know about
"Cons the Magnificent?"

3 #t.

Do you know what recursion is?

4 Absolutely.

What is a *goal*?

5 It is something that either *succeeds*, *fails*, or *has no value*.

#s is a goal that succeeds. What is #u[†]

6 Is it a goal that fails?

[†] #s is written `succeed` and #u is written `fail`. Each operator's index entry shows how that operator should be written. Also, see the inside front page for how to write various expressions from the book.

Exactly. What is the *value* of

```
(run* q
  #u)
```

7 (),
since #u fails, and because if *g* is a goal that fails, then the expression

```
(run* q g)
```

produces the empty list.

What is (≡ 'pea 'pod)

8 Is it also a goal?

Yes. Does the goal (≡† 'pea 'pod) succeed or fail?

9 It fails,
because pea is not the same as pod.

† ≡ is written == and is pronounced "equals."

Correct. What is the value of

```
(run* q
  (≡ 'pea 'pod))
```

10 (),
since the goal (≡ 'pea 'pod) fails.

What is the value of

```
(run* q
  (≡ q 'pea))
```

11 (pea).
The goal (≡ q 'pea) succeeds, *associating* pea with the *fresh* variable q.

If g is a goal that succeeds, then the expression

```
(run* q g)
```

produces a non-empty list of values associated with q.

Is the value of

```
(run* q
  (≡ 'pea q))
```

the same as the value of

```
(run* q
  (≡ q 'pea))
```

12 Yes, they both have the value (pea),
because the order of arguments to ≡ does not matter.

The First Law of ≡

(≡ v w) can be replaced by (≡ w v).

We use the phrase *what value is associated with* to mean the same thing as the phrase *what is the value of*, but with the outer parentheses removed from the resulting value. This lets us avoid one pair of matching parentheses when describing the value of a **run*** expression.

13 That's important to remember!

What value is associated with q in

```
(run* q
  (≡ 'pea q))
```

14 pea.
The value of the **run*** expression is (pea), and so the value associated with q is pea.

Does the variable q remain fresh in

```
(run* q
  (≡ 'pea q))
```

15 No.
In this expression q does not remain fresh because the value pea is associated with q.
We must mind our peas and qs.

Does the variable q remain fresh in

```
(run* q
  #s)
```

16 Yes.

Every variable is initially fresh. A variable is no longer fresh if it becomes associated with a non-variable value or if it becomes associated with a variable that, itself, is no longer fresh.

What is the value of

```
(run* q
  #s)
```

17 $(_{0})$.
In the value of a **run*** expression, each fresh variable is *reified* by appearing as the underscore symbol followed by a numeric subscript.

In the value $(_{0})$, what variable is reified as $_{0}$†

18 The fresh variable q.

† This symbol is written _0, and is created using (*reify-name* 0). We define *reify-name* in 10:93 (our notation for frame 93 of chapter 10).

What is the value of

```
(run* q
  (≡ 'pea 'pea))
```

19 $(_{0})$.
Although the **run*** expression produces a nonempty list, q remains fresh.

What is the value of

```
(run* q
  (≡ q q))
```

20 $(_{0})$.
Although the **run*** expression produces a nonempty list, the successful goal $(\equiv q\ q)$ does not associate any value with the variable q.

We can introduce a new fresh variable with **fresh**. What value is associated with *q* in

```
(run* q
  (fresh (x)
    (≡ 'pea q)))
```

21 pea.
Introducing an unused variable does not change the value associated with any other variable.

Is *x* the only variable that begins fresh in

```
(run* q
  (fresh (x)
    (≡ 'pea q)))
```

22 No,
since *q* also starts out fresh. All variables introduced by **fresh** or **run*** begin fresh.

Is *x* the only variable that remains fresh in

```
(run* q
  (fresh (x)
    (≡ 'pea q)))
```

23 Yes,
since pea is associated with *q*.

Suppose that we instead use *x* in the ≡ expression. What value is associated with *q* in

```
(run* q
  (fresh (x)
    (≡ 'pea x)))
```

24 $\_{0}$,
since *q* remains fresh.

Suppose that we use both *x* and *q*. What value is associated with *q* in

```
(run* q
  (fresh (x)
    (≡ (cons x '()) q)))
```

25 ($\_{0}$).
The value of (*cons* *x* '()) is associated with *q*, although *x* remains fresh.

What value is associated with q in

(run* q
  (fresh (x)
    $(\equiv$ `$(,x)$ q)))

26 $(\_{0})$,
since `$(,x)$ is a shorthand for $(cons\ x\ '())$.

Is this a bit subtle?

27 Indeed.

Commas (,), as in the **run*** expression in frame 26, can only precede variables. Thus, what is not a variable behaves as if it were quoted.

28 In that case, reading off the values of backtick (`) expressions should not be too difficult.

Two different fresh variables can be made the same by *fusing* them.

29 How can we fuse two different fresh variables?

We fuse two different fresh variables using $\equiv$. In the expression

(run* q
  (fresh (x)
    $(\equiv x\ q)$))

x and q are different fresh variables, so they are fused when the goal $(\equiv x\ q)$ succeeds.

30 Okay.

What value is associated with q in

(run* q
  (fresh (x)
    $(\equiv x\ q)$))

31 $\_{0}$.
x and q are fused, but remain fresh. Fused variables get the same association if a value (including another variable) is associated later with either variable.

What value is associated with q in

(run* q
  ($\equiv$ '(((pea)) pod) '(((pea)) pod)))

32 $\_{0}$.

What value is associated with *q* in

```
(run* q
  (≡ '(((pea)) pod) `(((pea)) ,q)))
```

33 pod.

What value is associated with *q* in

```
(run* q
  (≡ `(((,q)) pod) '(((pea)) pod)))
```

34 pea.

What value is associated with *q* in

```
(run* q
  (fresh (x)
    (≡ `(((,q)) pod) `(((,x)) pod))))
```

35 $\_{0}$,
since *q* remains fresh, even though *x* is fused with *q*.

What value is associated with *q* in

```
(run* q
  (fresh (x)
    (≡ `(((,q)) ,x) `(((,x)) pod))))
```

36 pod,
because pod is associated with *x*, and because *x* is fused with *q*.

What value is associated with *q* in

```
(run* q
  (fresh (x)
    (≡ `(,x ,x) q)))
```

37 $(\_{0}\ \_{0})$.
In the value of a **run*** expression, every instance of the same fresh variable is replaced by the same reified variable.

What value is associated with *q* in

```
(run* q
  (fresh (x)
    (fresh (y)
      (≡ `(,q ,y) `((,x ,y) ,x)))))
```

38 $(\_{0}\ \_{0})$,
because the value of `` `(,x ,y) `` is associated with *q*, and because *y* is fused with *x*, making *y* the same as *x*.

When are two variables *different*?

39 Two variables are different if they have not been fused.

Every variable introduced by **fresh** (or **run***) is initially different from every other variable.

Are *q* and *x* different variables in

```
(run* q
  (fresh (x)
    (≡ 'pea q)))
```

40 Yes, they are different.

What value is associated with *q* in

```
(run* q
  (fresh (x)
    (fresh (y)
      (≡ `(,x ,y) q))))
```

41 $(\_{0}\ \_{1})$.

In the value of a **run*** expression, each different fresh variable is reified with an underscore followed by a distinct numeric subscript.

What value is associated with *s* in

```
(run* s
  (fresh (t)
    (fresh (u)
      (≡ `(,t ,u) s))))
```

42 $(\_{0}\ \_{1})$.

This expression and the previous expression differ only in the names of their lexical variables. Such expressions have the same values.

What value is associated with *q* in

```
(run* q
  (fresh (x)
    (fresh (y)
      (≡ `(,x ,y ,x) q))))
```

43 $(\_{0}\ \_{1}\ \_{0})$.

x and *y* remain fresh, and since they are different variables, they are reified differently. Reified variables are indexed by the order they appear in the value produced by a **run*** expression.

Does

```
(≡ '(pea) 'pea)
```

succeed?

44 No, since (pea) is not the same as pea.

Does

(≡ \`(,x) x)

succeed if (pea pod) is associated with x

45 No, since ((pea pod)) is not the same as (pea pod).

Is there any value of x for which

(≡ \`(,x) x)

succeeds?

46 No.

But what if x were fresh?

Even then, (≡ \`(,x) x) could not succeed. No matter what value is associated with x, x cannot be equal to a list in which x *occurs*.

47 What does it mean for x to *occur*?

A variable x occurs in a variable y when x (or any variable fused with x) appears in the value associated with y.

48 When do we say a variable occurs in a list?

A variable x occurs in a list l when x (or any variable fused with x) is an element of l, or when x occurs in an element of l.

Does x occur in

\`(pea (,x) pod)

49 Yes, because x is in the value of \`(,x), the second element of the list.

The Second Law of ≡

If x is fresh, then (≡ v x) succeeds and associates v with x, unless x occurs in v.

What is the value of

(**run*** q
  ($conj_2$[†] #s #s))

[50] ($\_\_0$),
because the goal ($conj_2$ g_1 g_2) succeeds if the goals g_1 and g_2 both succeed.

† $conj_2$ is short for *two-argument conjunction*, and is written conj2.

What value is associated with q in

(**run*** q
  ($conj_2$ #s (≡ 'corn q)))

[51] corn,
because corn is associated with q when (≡ 'corn q) succeeds.

What is the value of

(**run*** q
  ($conj_2$ #u (≡ 'corn q)))

[52] (),
because the goal ($conj_2$ g_1 g_2) fails if g_1 fails.

Yes. The goal ($conj_2$ g_1 g_2) also fails if g_1 succeeds and g_2 fails.

What is the value of

(**run*** q
  ($conj_2$ (≡ 'corn q) (≡ 'meal q)))

[53] ().
In order for the $conj_2$ to succeed, (≡ 'corn q) and (≡ 'meal q) must both succeed. The first goal succeeds, associating corn with q. The second goal cannot then associate meal with q, since q is no longer fresh.

What is the value of

(**run*** q
  ($conj_2$ (≡ 'corn q) (≡ 'corn q)))

[54] (corn).
The first goal succeeds, associating corn with q. The second goal succeeds because although q is no longer fresh, the value associated with q is corn.

What is the value of

```
(run* q
  (disj₂† #u #u))
```

55 (),
because the goal $(disj_2\ g_1\ g_2)$ fails if both g_1 and g_2 fail.

† *disj₂* is short for *two-argument disjunction*, and is written disj2.

What is the value of

```
(run* q
  (disj₂ (≡ 'olive q) #u))
```

56 (olive),
because the goal $(disj_2\ g_1\ g_2)$ succeeds if either g_1 or g_2 succeeds.

What is the value of

```
(run* q
  (disj₂ #u (≡ 'oil q)))
```

57 (oil),
because the goal $(disj_2\ g_1\ g_2)$ succeeds if either g_1 or g_2 succeeds.

What is the value of

```
(run* q
  (disj₂ (≡ 'olive q) (≡ 'oil q)))
```

58 (olive oil), a list of two values.
Both goals contribute values. (≡ 'olive q) succeeds, and olive is the first value associated with q. (≡ 'oil q) also succeeds, and oil is the second value associated with q.

What is the value of

```
(run* q
  (fresh (x)
    (fresh (y)
      (disj₂
        (≡ `(,x ,y) q)
        (≡ `(,y ,x) q)))))
```

59 $((\_{0}\ \_{1})\ (\_{0}\ \_{1}))$,
because $disj_2$ contributes two values. In the first value, x is reified as $\_{0}$ and y is reified as $\_{1}$. In the second value, y is reified as $\_{0}$ and x is reified as $\_{1}$.

Correct!

The variables x and y are not fused in the previous **run*** expression, however. Each value produced by a **run*** expression is reified independently of any other values. This means that the numbering of reified variables begins again, from 0, within each reified value.

60 Okay.

Do we consider

```
(run* x
  (disj2 (≡ 'olive x) (≡ 'oil x)))
```

and

```
(run* x
  (disj2 (≡ 'oil x) (≡ 'olive x)))
```

to be the same?

61 Yes,

because the first **run*** expression produces (olive oil), the second **run*** expression produces (oil olive), and because the order of the values does *not* matter.

What is the value of

```
(run* x
  (disj2
    (conj2 (≡ 'olive x) #u)
    (≡ 'oil x)))
```

62 (oil).

What is the value of

```
(run* x
  (disj2
    (conj2 (≡ 'olive x) #s)
    (≡ 'oil x)))
```

63 (olive oil).

What is the value of

```
(run* x
  (disj2
    (≡ 'oil x)
    (conj2 (≡ 'olive x) #s)))
```

64 (oil olive).

65 What is the value of

```
(run* x
  (disj2
    (conj2 (≡ 'virgin x) #u)
    (disj2
      (≡ 'olive x)
      (disj2
        #s
        (≡ 'oil x)))))
```

(olive $\_{0}$ oil).
The goal (*conj₂* (≡ 'virgin x) #u) fails. Therefore, the body of the **run*** behaves the same as the second *disj₂*,

```
(disj2
  (≡ 'olive x)
  (disj2
    #s
    (≡ 'oil x))).
```

---

66 In the previous frame's expression, whose value is (olive $\_{0}$ oil), how do we end up with $\_{0}$

Through the #s in the innermost *disj₂*, which succeeds without associating a value with x.

---

67 What is the value of this **run*** expression?

```
(run* r
  (fresh (x)
    (fresh (y)
      (conj2
        (≡ 'split x)
        (conj2
          (≡ 'pea y)
          (≡ `(,x ,y) r))))))
```

((split pea)).

---

68 Is the value of this **run*** expression

```
(run* r
  (fresh (x)
    (fresh (y)
      (conj2
        (conj2
          (≡ 'split x)
          (≡ 'pea y))
        (≡ `(,x ,y) r)))))
```

the same as that of the previous frame?

Yes.

Can we make this **run*** expression shorter?

Is this,

```
(run* r
  (fresh (x)
    (fresh (y)
      (conj₂
        (conj₂
          (≡ 'split x)
          (≡ 'pea y))
        (≡ `(,x ,y) r)))))
```

shorter?

69 Very funny.

Is there another way to simplify this **run*** expression?

Yes. If **fresh** were able to create any number of variables, how might we rewrite the **run*** expression in the previous frame?

70 Like this,

```
(run* r
  (fresh (x y)
    (conj₂
      (conj₂
        (≡ 'split x)
        (≡ 'pea y))
      (≡ `(,x ,y) r)))).
```

Does the simplified expression in the previous frame still produce the value ((split pea))

71 Yes.

Can we keep simplifying this expression?

Sure. If **run*** were able to create any number of fresh variables, how might we rewrite the expression from frame 70?

72 As this simpler expression,

```
(run* (r x y)
  (conj₂
    (conj₂
      (≡ 'split x)
      (≡ 'pea y))
    (≡ `(,x ,y) r))).
```

Does the expression in the previous frame still produce the value ((split pea))

73 No.

The previous frame's **run*** expression produces (((split pea) split pea)), which is a list containing the values associated with r, x, and y, respectively.

How can we change the expression in frame 72 to get back the value from frame 70, ((split pea))

74 We can begin by removing r from the **run*** variable list.

Okay, so far. What else must we do, once we remove r from the **run*** variable list?

75 We must remove (≡ \`(,x ,y) r), which uses r, and the outer $conj_2$, since $conj_2$ expects two goals. Here is the new **run*** expression,

```
(run* (x y)
  (conj₂
    (≡ 'split x)
    (≡ 'pea y))).
```

What is the value of

```
(run* (x y)
  (disj₂
    (conj₂ (≡ 'split x) (≡ 'pea y))
    (conj₂ (≡ 'red x) (≡ 'bean y))))
```

76 The list ((split pea) (red bean)).

Good guess! What is the value of

```
(run* r
  (fresh (x y)
    (conj₂
      (disj₂
        (conj₂ (≡ 'split x) (≡ 'pea y))
        (conj₂ (≡ 'red x) (≡ 'bean y)))
      (≡ `(,x ,y soup) r))))
```

77 The list

((split pea soup) (red bean soup)).

Can we simplify this **run*** expression?

Yes. **fresh** can take two goals, in which case it acts like a $conj_2$.

How might we rewrite the **run*** expression in the previous frame?

78 Like this,

```
(run* r
  (fresh (x y)
    (disj2
      (conj2 (≡ 'split x) (≡ 'pea y))
      (conj2 (≡ 'red x) (≡ 'bean y)))
    (≡ `(,x ,y soup) r))).
```

Can **fresh** have more than two goals?

Yes.

Rewrite the **fresh** expression

```
(fresh (x ...)
  (conj2
    g1
    (conj2
      g2
      g3)))
```

to not use $conj_2$.

79 Can the expression be rewritten as

```
(fresh (x ...)
  g1
  g2
  g3)?
```

Yes, it can.

This expression produces the value ((split pea soup) (red bean soup)), just like the **run*** expression in frame 78.

```
(run* (x y z)
  (conj2
    (disj2
      (conj2 (≡ 'split x) (≡ 'pea y))
      (conj2 (≡ 'red x) (≡ 'bean y)))
    (≡ 'soup z)))
```

Can this **run*** expression be simplified?

80 Yes.

We can allow **run*** to have more than one goal and act like a $conj_2$, just as we did with **fresh**,

```
(run* (x y z)
  (disj2
    (conj2 (≡ 'split x) (≡ 'pea y))
    (conj2 (≡ 'red x) (≡ 'bean y)))
  (≡ 'soup z)).
```

How can we simplify this **run*** expression from frame 75?

```
(run* (x y)
  (conj₂
    (≡ 'split x)
    (≡ 'pea y)))
```

81 Like this,

```
(run* (x y)
  (≡ 'split x)
  (≡ 'pea y)).
```

Consider this very simple definition.

```
(defrel† (teacupᵒ t)
  (disj₂ (≡ 'tea t) (≡ 'cup t)))
```

The name **defrel** is short for *define relation.*

† The **defrel** form is implemented as a *macro* (page 177). We can write relations without **defrel** using **define** and two **lambda**s. See the right hand side for an example showing how *teacup*^{o} would be written.

82 What is a relation?

```
(define (teacupᵒ t)
  (lambda (s)
    (lambda ()
      ((disj₂ (≡ 'tea t) (≡ 'cup t))
       s)))).
```

When using **define** in this way, s is passed to the goal, ($disj_2$ ...). We have to ensure that s does not appear either in the goal expression itself, or as an argument (here, t) to the relation. Because hygienic macros avoid inadvertent variable capture, we do not have these problems when we use **defrel** instead of **define**. For more, see chapter 10 for implementation details.

A relation is a kind of function† that, when given arguments, produces a goal.

What is the value of

```
(run* x
  (teacupᵒ x))
```

† Thanks, Robert A. Kowalski (1941–).

83 (tea cup).

What is the value of

```
(run* (x y)
  (disj2
    (conj2 (teacupo† x) (≡ #t y))
    (conj2 (≡ #f x) (≡ #t y))))
```

† *teacup*^{o} is written `teacupo`. Henceforth, consult the index for how we write the names of relations.

84 ((#f #t) (tea #t) (cup #t)).†
First (≡ #f x) associates #f with x, then (*teacup*^{o} x) associates tea with x, and finally (*teacup*^{o} x) associates cup with x.

† Remember that the order of the values does not matter (see frame 61).

What is the value of

```
(run* (x y)
  (teacupo x)
  (teacupo y))
```

85 ((tea tea) (tea cup) (cup tea) (cup cup)).

What is the value of

```
(run* (x y)
  (teacupo x)
  (teacupo x))
```

86 ((tea $\_{0}$) (cup $\_{0}$)).
The first (*teacup*^{o} x) associates tea with x and then associates cup with x, while the second (*teacup*^{o} x) already has the correct associations for x, so it succeeds without associating anything. y remains fresh.

And what is the value of

```
(run* (x y)
  (disj2
    (conj2 (teacupo x) (teacupo x))
    (conj2 (≡ #f x) (teacupo y))))
```

87 ((#f tea) (#f cup) (tea $\_{0}$) (cup $\_{0}$)).

The **run*** expression in the previous frame has a pattern that appears frequently: a $disj_2$ containing $conj_2$s. This pattern appears so often that we introduce a new form, **cond**^{e}.†

```
(run* (x y)
  (conde
    ((teacupo x) (teacupo x))
    ((≡ #f x) (teacupo y))))
```

Revise the **run*** expression below, from frame 76, to use **cond**^{e} instead of $disj_2$ or $conj_2$.

```
(run* (x y)
  (disj2
    (conj2 (≡ 'split x) (≡ 'pea y))
    (conj2 (≡ 'red x) (≡ 'bean y))))
```

† **cond**^{e} is written conde and is pronounced "con-dee."

88 Here it is:

```
(run* (x y)
  (conde
    ((≡ 'split x) (≡ 'pea y))
    ((≡ 'red x) (≡ 'bean y)))).
```

---

cond^e can be used in place of $disj_2$, even when one of the goals in $disj_2$ is not a $conj_2$. Rewrite this **run*** expression from frame 62 to use **cond**^{e}.

```
(run* x
  (disj2
    (conj2 (≡ 'olive x) #u)
    (≡ 'oil x)))
```

89 Like this,

```
(run* x
  (conde
    ((≡ 'olive x) #u)
    ((≡ 'oil x)))).
```

What is the value of

```
(run* (x y)
  (conde
    ((fresh (z)
       (≡ 'lentil z)))
    ((≡ x y))))
```

90 $((\_{0}\ \_{1})\ (\_{0}\ \_{0}))$.
In the first **cond**^{e} line x remains different from y, and both are fresh. lentil is associated with z, which is not reified. In the second **cond**^{e} line, both x and y remain fresh, but x is fused with y.

We can extend the number of lines in a **cond**^{e}. What is the value of

```
(run* (x y)
  (conde
    ((≡ 'split x) (≡ 'pea y))
    ((≡ 'red x) (≡ 'bean y))
    ((≡ 'green x) (≡ 'lentil y))))
```

91 ((split pea) (red bean) (green lentil)).

Does that mean $disj_2$ and $conj_2$ are unnecessary?

Correct. We won't see $disj_2$ or $conj_2$ again until we go "Under the Hood" in chapter 10.

92 What does the "*e*" in **cond**^{e} stand for?

It stands for *every*, since every successful **cond**^{e} line contributes one or more values.

93 Hmm, interesting.

The Law of cond^e

Every *successful* cond^e line contributes one or more values.

⟹ Now go make an almond butter and jam sandwich. ⟸

This space reserved for

JAM STAINS!

2.
Teaching Old Toys New Tricks

What is the value of

```
(car '(grape raisin pear))
```

1 grape.

What is the value of

```
(car '(a c o r n))
```

2 a.

What value is associated with *q* in

```
(run* q
  (car° '(a c o r n) q))
```

3 a,
because a is the *car* of (a c o r n).

What value is associated with *q* in

```
(run* q
  (car° '(a c o r n) 'a))
```

4 $\_{0}$,
because a is the *car* of (a c o r n).

What value is associated with *r* in

```
(run* r
  (fresh (x y)
    (car° `(,r ,y) x)
    (≡ 'pear x)))
```

5 pear.
Since the *car* of `(,r ,y), which is the fresh variable *r*, is fused with *x*. Then pear is associated with *x*, which in turn associates pear with *r*.

Here is *car*°.

```
(defrel (car° p a)
  (fresh (d)
    (≡ (cons a d) p)))
```

What is unusual about this definition?

6 Whereas *car* expects one argument, *car*° expects two.

What is the value of

```
(cons
  (car '(grape raisin pear))
  (car '((a) (b) (c))))
```

7 That's familiar: (grape a).

What value is associated with r in

```
(run* r
  (fresh (x y)
    (car° '(grape raisin pear) x)
    (car° '((a) (b) (c)) y)
    (≡ (cons x y) r)))
```

8 The same value: (grape a).

Why can we use *cons* in the previous frame?

9 Because variables introduced by **fresh** *are* values, and each argument to *cons* can be any value.

What is the value of

```
(cdr '(grape raisin pear))
```

10 Another familiar one: (raisin pear).

What is the value of

```
(car (cdr (cdr '(a c o r n))))
```

11 o.

What value is associated with r in

```
(run* r
  (fresh (v)
    (cdr° '(a c o r n) v)
    (fresh (w)
      (cdr° v w)
      (car° w r))))
```

12 o.

The process of transforming (*car* (*cdr* (*cdr* l))) into (*cdr*° l v), (*cdr*° v w), and (*car*° w r) is called *unnesting*. We introduce **fresh** expressions as necessary as we unnest.

Define *cdr*°.

13 It is *almost* the same as *car*°.

```
(defrel (cdr° p d)
  (fresh (a)
    (≡ (cons a d) p)))
```

What is the value of

```
(cons
  (cdr '(grape raisin pear))
  (car '((a) (b) (c))))
```

14 Also familiar: ((raisin pear) a).

What value is associated with *r* in

```
(run* r
  (fresh (x y)
    (cdr° '(grape raisin pear) x)
    (car° '((a) (b) (c)) y)
    (≡ (cons x y) r)))
```

15 That's the same: ((raisin pear) a).

What value is associated with *q* in

```
(run* q
  (cdr° '(a c o r n) '(c o r n)))
```

16 _0,
because (c o r n) is the *cdr* of (a c o r n).

What value is associated with *x* in

```
(run* x
  (cdr° '(c o r n) `(,x r n)))
```

17 o,
because (o r n) is the *cdr* of (c o r n), so o is associated with *x*.

What value is associated with *l* in

```
(run* l
  (fresh (x)
    (cdr° l '(c o r n))
    (car° l x)
    (≡ 'a x)))
```

18 (a c o r n),
because if the *cdr* of *l* is (c o r n), then the list `(,*a* c o r n) is associated with *l*, where *a* is the variable introduced in the definition of *cdr°*. The *car°* of *l*, *a*, fuses with *x*. When we associate a with *x*, we also associate a with *a*, so the list (a c o r n) is associated with *l*.

What value is associated with *l* in

```
(run* l
  (cons° '(a b c) '(d e) l))
```

19 ((a b c) d e),
since *cons°* associates the value of (*cons* '(a b c) '(d e)) with *l*.

What value is associated with x in

```
(run* x
  (conso x '(a b c) '(d a b c)))
```

20 d.

Since (*cons* 'd '(a b c)) is (d a b c), $cons^o$ associates d with x.

What value is associated with r in

```
(run* r
  (fresh (x y z)
    (≡ `(e a d ,x) r)
    (conso y `(a ,z c) r)))
```

21 (e a d c).

We first associate `(e a d ,x) with r. We then perform the $cons^o$, associating c with x, d with z, and e with y.

What value is associated with x in

```
(run* x
  (conso x `(a ,x c) `(d a ,x c)))
```

22 d,

the value we can associate with x so that (*cons* x `(a ,x c)) is `(d a ,x c).

What value is associated with l in

```
(run* l
  (fresh (x)
    (≡ `(d a ,x c) l)
    (conso x `(a ,x c) l)))
```

23 (d a d c).

First we associate `(d a ,x c) with $l$. Then when we $cons^o$ $x$ to `(a ,x c), we associate d with x.

What value is associated with l in

```
(run* l
  (fresh (x)
    (conso x `(a ,x c) l)
    (≡ `(d a ,x c) l)))
```

24 (d a d c), as in the previous frame.

We $cons^o$ x to `(a ,x c), associating the list `(,x a ,x c) with l. Then when we associate `(d a ,x c) with l, we associate d with x.

Define $cons^o$ using car^o and cdr^o.

25 Here is a definition.

```
(defrel (conso a d p)
  (caro p a)
  (cdro p d))
```

26 Now, define the $cons^o$ relation using $\equiv$ instead of car^o and cdr^o.

Here is the new $cons^o$.

```
(defrel (conso a d p)
  (≡ `(,a . ,d) p))
```

27 Here's a bonus question.

What value is associated with l in

```
(run* l
  (fresh (d t x y w)
    (conso w '(n u s) t)
    (cdro l t)
    (caro l x)
    (≡ 'b x)
    (cdro l d)
    (caro d y)
    (≡ 'o y)))
```

It's a five-element list.[†]

[†] t is (*cdr* l) and since l is fresh, (cdr^o l t) places a fresh variable in the (*car* l), while associating (*car* t) with w; (*car* l) is the fresh variable x; b is associated with x; t is associated with d and the *car* of d is associated with y, which fuses w with y; and the last step associates o with y.

28 What is the value of

```
(null? '(grape raisin pear))
```

#f.

29 What is the value of

```
(null? '())
```

#t.

30 What is the value of

```
(run* q
  (nullo '(grape raisin pear)))
```

().

31 What is the value of

```
(run* q
  (nullo '()))
```

($\_{0}$).

What is the value of

(**run*** x
  ($null^o$ x))

[32] (()),
since the only way ($null^o$ x) succeeds is if the empty list, (), is associated with x.

Define $null^o$ using ≡.

[33] Here is $null^o$.

(**defrel** ($null^o$ x)
  (≡ '() x))

Is (split . pea) a pair?

[34] Yes.

Is \`(split . ,x) a pair?

[35] Yes.

What is the value of

(*pair?* '((split) . pea))

[36] #t.

What is the value of

(*pair?* '())

[37] #f.

Is pair a pair?

[38] No.

Is pear a pair?

[39] No.

Is (pear) a pair?

[40] Yes,
it is the pair (pear . ()).

What is the value of (*car* '(pear))	41 pear.
What is the value of (*cdr* '(pear))	42 ().
How can we build these pairs?	43 Use *Cons the Magnificent.*
What is the value of (*cons* '(split) 'pea)	44 ((split) . pea).

What value is associated with r in
(**run*** r
  (**fresh** (x y)
    ($\equiv$ (*cons* x (*cons* y 'salad)) r)))
	45 ($\_{0}$ $\_{1}$. salad).

Here is *pair*^{o}.
(**defrel** (*pair*^{o} p)
  (**fresh** (a d)
    (*cons*^{o} a d p)))
Is *pair*^{o} recursive?
	46 No, it is not.

What is the value of (**run*** q (*pair*^{o} (*cons* q q)))	47 ($\_{0}$). (*cons* q q) creates a pair of the same fresh variable. But we are not interested in the pair, only q.

What is the value of

```
(run* q
  (pair^o '()))
```

48 ().

What is the value of

```
(run* q
  (pair^o 'pair))
```

49 ().

What value is associated with x in

```
(run* x
  (pair^o x))
```

50 $(\_{0} \cdot \_{1})$.

What value is associated with r in

```
(run* r
  (pair^o (cons r '())))
```

51 $\_{0}$.

Is (tofu) a *singleton*?

52 Yes,
because it is a list of a single value, tofu.

Is ((tofu)) a singleton?

53 Yes,
because it is a list of a single value, (tofu).

Is tofu a singleton?

54 No,
because it is not a list of a single value.

Is (e tofu) a singleton?

55 No,
because it is not a list of a single value.

Is () a singleton?

56 No,
because it is not a list of a single value.

Is (e . tofu) a singleton?

57 No,
because (e . tofu) is not a list of a single value.

Consider the definition of *singleton?*.

```
(define (singleton? l)
  (cond
    ((pair? l) (null? (cdr l)))
    (else #f)))
```

What is the value of

(*singleton?* '((a) (a b) c))

58 #f.

---

singleton? determines if its argument is a *proper list* of length one.

59 What is a proper list?

A list is *proper* if it is the empty list or if it is a pair whose *cdr* is proper.

What is the value of

(*singleton?* '())

60 #f.

What is the value of

(*singleton?* (*cons* 'pea '()))

61 #t,
because (pea) is a proper list of length one.

What is the value of

(*singleton?* '(sauerkraut))

62 #t.

To translate *singleton?* into *singleton*^{o}, we must replace **else** with #t in the last **cond** line.

63 Like this.

```
(define (singleton? l)
  (cond
    ((pair? l) (null? (cdr l)))
    (#t #f)))
```

Here is the translation of *singleton?*.

```
(defrel (singletonᵒ l)
  (condᵉ
    ((pairᵒ l)
     (fresh (d)
       (cdrᵒ l d)
       (nullᵒ d)))
    (#s #u)))
```

Is *singleton*^{o} a correct definition?

64 It looks correct.

How do we translate a function into a relation?

The Translation (Initial)

To translate a function into a relation, first replace define with defrel. Then unnest each expression in each cond line, and replace each cond with cond^e**. To unnest a #t, replace it with #s. To unnest a #f, replace it with #u.**

Where does

```
(fresh (d)
  (cdrᵒ l d)
  (nullᵒ d))
```

come from?

65 It is an unnesting of (*null?* (*cdr* *l*)). First we determine the *cdr* of *l* and associate it with the fresh variable *d*, and then we translate *null?* to *null*^{o}.

66 Any **cond**^{e} line that has a top-level #u as a goal cannot contribute values.

Simplify *singleton*^{o}.

Here it is.

```
(defrel (singletonᵒ l)
  (condᵉ
    ((pairᵒ l)
     (fresh (d)
       (cdrᵒ l d)
       (nullᵒ d)))))
```

The Law of #u

Any cond^e line that has #u as a top-level goal cannot contribute values.

67 Do we need (*pair*^{o} *l*) in the definition of *singleton*^{o}

No.
This **cond**^{e} line also uses (*cdr*^{o} *l* *d*). If *d* is fresh, then (*pair*^{o} *l*) succeeds exactly when (*cdr*^{o} *l* *d*) succeeds. So here (*pair*^{o} *l*) is unnecessary.

68 After we remove (*pair*^{o} *l*), the **cond**^{e} has only one goal in its only line. We can also replace the whole **cond**^{e} with just this goal.

What is our newly simplified definition of *singleton*^{o}

It's even shorter!

```
(defrel (singletonᵒ l)
  (fresh (d)
    (cdrᵒ l d)
    (nullᵒ d)))
```

⟹ Define both *car*^{o} and *cdr*^{o} using *cons*^{o}. ⟸

3.
Seeing Old Friends in New Ways

Consider the definition of *list?*, where we have replaced **else** with #t.

```
(define (list? l)
  (cond
    ((null? l) #t)
    ((pair? l) (list? (cdr l)))
    (#t #f)))
```

From now on we assume that each **else** has been replaced by #t.

What is the value of

(*list?* '((a) (a b) c))

1 #t.

What is the value of

(*list?* '())

2 #t.

What is the value of

(*list?* 's)

3 #f.

What is the value of

(*list?* '(d a t e . s))

4 #f,
because (d a t e . s) is not a proper list.

Translate *list?*.

5 This is almost the same as *singleton*^{o}.

```
(defrel (listᵒ l)
  (condᵉ
    ((nullᵒ l) #s)
    ((pairᵒ l)
     (fresh (d)
       (cdrᵒ l d)
       (listᵒ d)))
    (#s #u)))
```

Where does

```
(fresh (d)
  (cdr° l d)
  (list° d))
```

come from?

6 It is an unnesting of (*list?* (*cdr* *l*)). First we determine the *cdr* of *l* and associate it with the fresh variable *d*, and then we use *d* as the argument in the recursion.

Here is a simplified version of *list°*. What simplifications have we made?

```
(defrel (list° l)
  (condᵉ
    ((null° l) #s)
    ((fresh (d)
       (cdr° l d)
       (list° d)))))
```

7 We have removed the final **cond**^{e} line, because **The Law of #u** says **cond**^{e} lines that have #u as a top-level goal cannot contribute values. We also have removed (*pair°* *l*), as in frame 2:68.

Can we simplify *list°* further?

Yes, since any top-level #s can be removed from a **cond**^{e} line.

8 Here is our simplified version.

```
(defrel (list° l)
  (condᵉ
    ((null° l))
    ((fresh (d)
       (cdr° l d)
       (list° d)))))
```

The Law of #s

Any top-level #s can be removed from a cond^e line.

What is the value of

(**run*** x
  (*list*^{o} \`(a b ,x d)))

where a, b, and d are symbols, and x is a variable?

9 ($\_0$),
since x remains fresh.

Why is ($\_0$) the value of

(**run*** x
  (*list*^{o} \`(a b ,x d)))

10 For this use of *list*^{o} to succeed, it is not necessary to determine the value of x. Therefore x remains fresh, which shows that this use of *list*^{o} succeeds *for any* value associated with x.

How is ($\_0$) the value of

(**run*** x
  (*list*^{o} \`(a b ,x d)))

11 *list*^{o} gets the *cdr* of each pair, and then uses recursion on that *cdr*. When *list*^{o} reaches the end of \`(a b ,x d), it succeeds because (*null*^{o} '()) succeeds, thus leaving x fresh.

What is the value of

(**run*** x
  (*list*^{o} \`(a b c . ,x)))

12 This expression has *no value.*
Aren't there an unbounded number of possible values that could be associated with x?

Yes, that's why it has no value. We can use **run** 1 to get a list of only the first value. Describe **run**'s behavior.

13 Along with the arguments **run*** expects, **run** also expects a positive number n. If the **run** expression has a value, its value is a list of at most n elements.

What is the value of

(**run** 1 x
  (*list*^{o} \`(a b c . ,x)))

14 (()).

What value is associated with x in

(**run** 1 x
  ($list^o$ \`(a b c . ,x)))

15 ().

Why is () the value associated with x in

(**run** 1 x
  ($list^o$ \`(a b c . ,x)))

16 Because \`(a b c . ,x) is a proper list when x is the empty list.

How is () the value associated with x in

(**run** 1 x
  ($list^o$ \`(a b c . ,x)))

17 When $list^o$ reaches the end of \`(a b c . ,x), ($null^o$ x) succeeds and associates x with the empty list.

What is the value of

(**run** 5 x
  ($list^o$ \`(a b c . ,x)))†

† As we state in frame 1:61, the order of values is unimportant. This **run** gives the first five values under an ordering determined by the $list^o$ relation. We see how the implementation produces these values in particular when we discover how the implementation works in chapter 10.

18 (()
 ($\_0$)
 ($\_0$ $\_1$)
 ($\_0$ $\_1$ $\_2$)
 ($\_0$ $\_1$ $\_2$ $\_3$)).

Why are the nonempty values lists of ($\_n$)

19 Each $\_n$ corresponds to a fresh variable that has been introduced in the goal of the second **cond**^{e} line of $list^o$.

We need one more example to understand **run**. In frame 1:91 we use **run*** to produce all three values. How many values would be produced with **run** 7 instead of **run***

20 The same three values,

((split pea) (red bean) (green lentil)).

Does that mean if **run*** produces a list, then **run** n either produces the same list, or a prefix of that list?

---

21 Yes. Here is *lol?*, where *lol?* stands for *list-of-lists?*.

```
(define (lol? l)
  (cond
    ((null? l) #t)
    ((list? (car l)) (lol? (cdr l)))
    (#t #f)))
```

Describe what *lol?* does.

As long as each top-level value in the list *l* is a proper list, *lol?* produces #t. Otherwise, *lol?* produces #f.

---

22 Here is the translation of *lol?*.

```
(defrel (lolᵒ l)
  (condᵉ
    ((nullᵒ l) #s)
    ((fresh (a)
       (carᵒ l a)
       (listᵒ a))
     (fresh (d)
       (cdrᵒ l d)
       (lolᵒ d)))
    (#s #u)))
```

Simplify *lol*^{o} using **The Law of #u** and **The Law of #s.**

Here it is.

```
(defrel (lolᵒ l)
  (condᵉ
    ((nullᵒ l))
    ((fresh (a)
       (carᵒ l a)
       (listᵒ a))
     (fresh (d)
       (cdrᵒ l d)
       (lolᵒ d)))))
```

---

23 What value is associated with q in

```
(run* q
  (fresh (x y)
    (lolᵒ `((a b) (,x c) (d ,y)))))
```

$\_{0}$,
since `((a b) (,x c) (d ,y)) is a list of lists.

---

24 What is the value of

```
(run 1 l
  (lolᵒ l))
```

(()).
Since *l* is fresh, (*null*^{o} *l*) succeeds and associates () with *l*.

What value is associated with q in

(**run** 1 q
  (**fresh** (x)
    (lol^o `((a b) . ,x))))

25 $\_{0}$,
because $null^o$ of a fresh variable always succeeds and associates () with the fresh variable x.

What is the value of

(**run** 1 x
  (lol^o `((a b) (c d) . ,x)))

26 (()),
since replacing x with the empty list in `((a b) (c d) . ,x) transforms it to ((a b) (c d) . ()), which is the same as ((a b) (c d)).

What is the value of

(**run** 5 x
  (lol^o `((a b) (c d) . ,x)))

27 (()
 (())
 (($\_{0}$))
 (() ())
 (($\_{0}$ $\_{1}$))).

What do we get when we replace x in

`((a b) (c d) . ,x)

by the fourth list in the previous frame?

28 ((a b) (c d) . (() ())),
which is the same as
((a b) (c d) () ()).

What is the value of

(**run** 5 x
  (lol^o x))

29 (()
 (())
 (($\_{0}$))
 (() ())
 (($\_{0}$ $\_{1}$))).

Is ((g) (tofu)) a list of singletons?

30 Yes,
since both (g) and (tofu) are singletons.

31 Is ((g) (e tofu)) a list of singletons?

No,
since (e tofu) is not a singleton.

---

32 Recall our definition of *singleton*^{o} from frame 2:68.

```
(defrel (singletonᵒ l)
  (fresh (d)
    (cdrᵒ l d)
    (nullᵒ d)))
```

Redefine *singleton*^{o} without using *cdr*^{o} or *null*^{o}.

Here it is.

```
(defrel (singletonᵒ l)
  (fresh (a)
    (≡ `(,a) l)))
```

---

33 Define *los*^{o}, where *los*^{o} stands for list of singletons.

Is this correct?

```
(defrel (losᵒ l)
  (condᵉ
    ((nullᵒ l))
    ((fresh (a)
       (carᵒ l a)
       (singletonᵒ a))
     (fresh (d)
       (cdrᵒ l d)
       (losᵒ d)))))
```

---

34 Let's try it out. What value is associated with z in

```
(run 1 z
  (losᵒ `((g) . ,z)))
```

().

---

35 Why is () the value associated with z in

```
(run 1 z
  (losᵒ `((g) . ,z)))
```

Because `((g) . ,z) is a list of singletons when z is the empty list.

What do we get when we replace *z* in

```
`((g) . ,z)
```

by ()

36 ((g) . ()),

which is the same as ((g)).

How is () the value associated with *z* in

```
(run 1 z
  (los° `((g) . ,z)))
```

37 The variable *l* from the definition of *los°* starts out as the list \`((g) . ,*z*). Since this list is not null, (*null° l*) fails and we determine the values contributed from the second **cond**$^e$ line. In the second **cond**$^e$ line, *d* is fused with *z*, the *cdr* of \`((g) . ,*z*). The variable *d* is then passed in the recursion. Since the variables *d* and *z* are fresh, (*null° l*) succeeds and associates () with *d* and *z*.

What is the value of

```
(run 5 z
  (los° `((g) . ,z)))
```

38

```
(()
 ((_0))
 ((_0) (_1))
 ((_0) (_1) (_2))
 ((_0) (_1) (_2) (_3))).
```

Why are the nonempty values ($\_n$)

39 Each $\_n$ corresponds to a fresh variable *a* that has been introduced in the first goal of the second **cond**^{e} line of *los°*.

What do we get when we replace *z* in

```
`((g) . ,z)
```

by the fourth list in frame 38?

40 ((g) . ((_0) (_1) (_2))),

which is the same as

((g) (_0) (_1) (_2)).

What is the value of

```
(run 4 r
  (fresh (w x y z)
    (los° `((g) (e . ,w) (,x . ,y) . ,z))
    (≡ `(,w (,x . ,y) ,z) r)))
```

41

```
((() (_0) ())
 (() (_0) ((_1)))
 (() (_0) ((_1) (_2)))
 (() (_0) ((_1) (_2) (_3)))).
```

42 What do we get when we replace *w*, *x*, *y*, and *z* in

```
`((g) (e . ,w) (,x . ,y) . ,z)
```

using the third list in the previous frame?

```
((g) (e) (_0) . ((_1) (_2))),
```

which is the same as

```
((g) (e) (_0) (_1) (_2)).
```

---

43 What is the value of

```
(run 3 out
  (fresh (w x y z)
    (≡ `((g) (e . ,w) (,x . ,y) . ,z) out)
    (los° out)))
```

```
(((g) (e) (_0))
 ((g) (e) (_0) (_1))
 ((g) (e) (_0) (_1) (_2))).
```

---

44 Remember *member?*.

```
(define (member? x l)
  (cond
    ((null? l) #f)
    ((equal? (car l) x) #t)
    (#t (member? x (cdr l)))))
```

What is the value of

```
(member? 'olive '(virgin olive oil))
```

#t.

---

45 Try to translate *member?*.

Is this *member°* correct?

```
(defrel (member° x l)
  (condᵉ
    ((null° l) #u)
    ((fresh (a)
       (car° l a)
       (≡ a x))
     #s)
    (#s
     (fresh (d)
       (cdr° l d)
       (member° x d)))))
```

Yes, because *equal?* unnests to ≡.

Simplify *member°* using **The Law of #u** and **The Law of #s**.

46 This is a simpler definition.

```
(defrel (memberᵒ x l)
  (condᵉ
    ((fresh (a)
       (carᵒ l a)
       (≡ a x)))
    ((fresh (d)
       (cdrᵒ l d)
       (memberᵒ x d)))))
```

Is this a simplification of *member°*

```
(defrel (memberᵒ x l)
  (condᵉ
    ((carᵒ l x))
    ((fresh (d)
       (cdrᵒ l d)
       (memberᵒ x d)))))
```

47 Yes,

since in the previous frame (≡ *a x*) fuses *a* with *x*. Therefore (*car° l a*) is the same as (*car° l x*).

What value is associated with *q* in

```
(run* q
  (memberᵒ 'olive '(virgin olive oil)))
```

48 _0,

because the use of *member°* succeeds, but this is still uninteresting; the only variable *q* is not used in the body of the **run*** expression.

What value is associated with *y* in

```
(run 1 y
  (memberᵒ y '(hummus with pita)))
```

49 hummus,

because the first **condᵉ** line in *member°* associates the value of (*car l*), which is hummus, with the fresh variable *y*.

What value is associated with *y* in

```
(run 1 y
  (memberᵒ y '(with pita)))
```

50 with,

because the first **condᵉ** line associates the value of (*car l*), which is with, with the fresh variable *y*.

What value is associated with *y* in

```
(run 1 y
  (memberᵒ y '(pita)))
```

51 pita,
because the first **cond**^{e} line associates the value of (*car l*), which is pita, with the fresh variable *y*.

What is the value of

```
(run* y
  (memberᵒ y '()))
```

52 (),
because neither **cond**^{e} line succeeds.

What is the value of

```
(run* y
  (memberᵒ y '(hummus with pita)))
```

53 (hummus with pita).
We already know the value of each recursion of *member*^{o}, provided *y* is fresh.

So is the value of

```
(run* y
  (memberᵒ y l))
```

always the value of *l*

54 Yes, when *l* is a proper list.

What is the value of

```
(run* y
  (memberᵒ y l))
```

where *l* is (pear grape . peaches)

55 (pear grape).
y is not the same as *l* in this case, since *l* is not a proper list.

What valuc is associated with *x* in

```
(run* x
  (memberᵒ 'e `(pasta ,x fagioli)))
```

56 e.
The list contains three values with a variable in the middle. *member*^{o} determines that e is associated with *x*.

Why is e the value associated with *x* in

```
(run* x
  (memberᵒ 'e `(pasta ,x fagioli)))
```

57 Because e is the only value that can be associated with *x* so that

```
(memberᵒ 'e `(pasta ,x fagioli))
```

succeeds.

What have we just done?

58 We filled in a blank in the list so that *member*^{o} succeeds.

What value is associated with x in

```
(run 1 x
  (membero 'e `(pasta e ,x fagioli)))
```

59 $\_{0}$,

because the recursion reaches e, and succeeds, *before* it gets to x.

What value is associated with x in

```
(run 1 x
  (membero 'e `(pasta ,x e fagioli)))
```

60 e,

because the recursion reaches the variable x, and succeeds, *before* it gets to e.

What is the value of

```
(run* (x y)
  (membero 'e `(pasta ,x fagioli ,y)))
```

61 ((e $\_{0}$) ($\_{0}$ e)).

What does each value in the list mean?

62 There are two values in the list. We know from frame 60 that for the first value when e is associated with x, (*member*^{o} 'e `(pasta ,x fagioli ,y)) succeeds, leaving y fresh. Then we determine the second value. Here, e is associated with y, while leaving x fresh.

What is the value of

```
(run* q
  (fresh (x y)
    (≡ `(pasta ,x fagioli ,y) q)
    (membero 'e q)))
```

63 ((pasta e fagioli $\_{0}$) (pasta $\_{0}$ fagioli e)).

What is the value of

```
(run 1 l
  (membero 'tofu l))
```

64 ((tofu . $\_{0}$)).

Which lists are represented by (tofu . $\_{0}$)

65 Every list whose *car* is tofu.

What is the value of

```
(run* l
  (memberᵒ 'tofu l))
```

66 It has no value,
because **run*** never finishes building the list.

What is the value of

```
(run 5 l
  (memberᵒ 'tofu l))
```

67 ((tofu . $\_{0}$)
($\_{0}$ tofu . $\_{1}$)
($\_{0}$ $\_{1}$ tofu . $\_{2}$)
($\_{0}$ $\_{1}$ $\_{2}$ tofu . $\_{3}$)
($\_{0}$ $\_{1}$ $\_{2}$ $\_{3}$ tofu . $\_{4}$)).

tofu is in every list.

But can we require each list containing tofu to be a proper list, instead of having a dot before each list's final reified variable?

Perhaps. This final reified variable appears in each value just after we find tofu. In *member*^{o}, which **cond**^{e} line associates tofu with the *car* of a pair?

68 The first line, ((*car*^{o} *l* *x*)).

What does *member*^{o}'s first **cond**^{e} line say about the *cdr* of *l*

69 Nothing. This is why the final *cdr*s remain fresh in frame 67.

If the *cdr* of *l* is (), is *l* a proper list?

70 Yes.

If the *cdr* of *l* is (beet), is *l* a proper list?

71 Yes.

Suppose *l* is a proper list. What values could be *l*'s *cdr*

72 Any proper list.

Here is *proper-member*^{o}.

```
(defrel (proper-memberᵒ x l)
  (condᵉ
    ((carᵒ l x)
     (fresh (d)
       (cdrᵒ l d)
       (listᵒ d)))
    ((fresh (d)
       (cdrᵒ l d)
       (proper-memberᵒ x d)))))
```

Do *proper-member*^{o} and *member*^{o} differ?

73 Yes. The *cdr* of *l* in the first **cond**^{e} line of *proper-member*^{o} must be a proper list.

Now what is the value of

```
(run 12 l
  (proper-memberᵒ 'tofu l))
```

74 Every list is proper.

```
((tofu)
 (tofu _0)
 (tofu _0 _1)
 (_0 tofu)
 (tofu _0 _1 _2)
 (tofu _0 _1 _2 _3)
 (_0 tofu _1)
 (tofu _0 _1 _2 _3 _4)
 (tofu _0 _1 _2 _3 _4 _5)
 (_0 tofu _1 _2)
 (tofu _0 _1 _2 _3 _4 _5 _6)
 (_0 _1 tofu)).
```

Is there a function *proper-member?* we can transform and simplify into *proper-member*^{o}

75 Yes. And here it is.

```
(define (proper-member? x l)
  (cond
    ((null? l) #f)
    ((equal? (car l) x) (list? (cdr l)))
    (#t (proper-member? x (cdr l)))))
```

$\Longrightarrow$ Now go make a cashew butter and marmalade sandwich $\Longleftarrow$
$\Longrightarrow$ and eat it! $\Longleftarrow$

This space reserved for **MARMALADE STAINS!**

4. Double Your Fun

Here is *append*.†

```
(define (append l t)
  (cond
    ((null? l) t)
    (#t (cons (car l)
          (append (cdr l) t)))))
```

What is the value of
(*append* '(a b c) '(d e))

1 (a b c d e).

† For a different approach to *append*, see William F. Clocksin. *Clause and Effect.* Springer, 1997, page 59.

What is the value of
(*append* '(a b c) '())

2 (a b c).

What is the value of
(*append* '() '(d e))

3 (d e).

What is the value of
(*append* 'a '(d e))

4 It has no meaning, because a is not a proper list.

What is the value of
(*append* '(d e) 'a)

5 It has no meaning, again?

No. The value is (d e . a).

6 How is that possible?

Look closely at the definition of *append*.

7 There are no **cond**-line questions asked about *t*. Ouch.

Here is the translation from *append* and its simplification to $append^o$.

```
(defrel (appendᵒ l t out)
  (condᵉ
    ((nullᵒ l) (≡ t out))
    ((fresh (res)
       (fresh (d)
         (cdrᵒ l d)
         (appendᵒ d t res))
       (fresh (a)
         (carᵒ l a)
         (consᵒ a res out))))))
```

How does $append^o$ differ from $list^o$, lol^o, and $member^o$

8 The *list?*, *lol?*, and *member?* definitions from the previous chapter have only Booleans as their values. *append*, on the other hand, has more interesting values.

Are there consequences of this difference?

Yes, we introduce an additional argument, which here we call *out*, that holds the value that would have been produced by *append*'s value.

9 That's like car^o, cdr^o, and $cons^o$, which also take an additional argument.

The Translation (Final)

To translate a function into a relation, first replace define with defrel. Then unnest each expression in each cond line, and replace each cond with cond^e. To unnest a #t, replace it with #s. To unnest a #f, replace it with #u.

If the value of at least one cond line can be a *non*-Boolean, add an argument, say *out*, to defrel to hold what would have been the function's value. When unnesting a line whose value is not a Boolean, ensure that either some value is associated with *out*, or that *out* is the last argument to a recursion.

Why are there three **fresh**es in

```
(fresh (res)
  (fresh (d)
    (cdrᵒ l d)
    (appendᵒ d t res))
  (fresh (a)
    (carᵒ l a)
    (consᵒ a res out)))
```

10 Because *d* is only mentioned in (*cdr*ᵒ *l d*) and (*append*ᵒ *d t res*); *a* is only mentioned in (*car*ᵒ *l a*) and (*cons*ᵒ *a res out*). But *res* is mentioned in both inner **fresh**es.

Rewrite

```
(fresh (res)
  (fresh (d)
    (cdrᵒ l d)
    (appendᵒ d t res))
  (fresh (a)
    (carᵒ l a)
    (consᵒ a res out)))
```

using only one **fresh**.

11
```
(fresh (a d res)
  (cdrᵒ l d)
  (appendᵒ d t res)
  (carᵒ l a)
  (consᵒ a res out)).
```

How might we use *cons*ᵒ in place of the *cdr*ᵒ and the *car*ᵒ

12
```
(fresh (a d res)
  (consᵒ a d l)
  (appendᵒ d t res)
  (consᵒ a res out)).
```

Redefine *append*ᵒ using these simplifications.

13 Here it is.

```
(defrel (appendᵒ l t out)
  (condᵉ
    ((nullᵒ l) (≡ t out))
    ((fresh (a d res)
       (consᵒ a d l)
       (appendᵒ d t res)
       (consᵒ a res out)))))
```

Can we similarly simplify our definitions of *los*^{o} as in frame 3:33, *lol*^{o} as in frame 3:22, and *proper-member*^{o} as in frame 3:73?

14 Yes.

In our simplified definition of *append*^{o}, how does the first *cons*^{o} differ from the second one?

15 The first *cons*^{o},

```
(conso a d l),
```

appears to associate values with the variables *a* and *d*. In other words, it appears to take apart a *cons* pair, whereas

```
(conso a res out)
```

appears to build a *cons* pair.

But, can appearances be deceiving?

16 Indeed they can.

What is the value of

```
(run 6 x
  (fresh (y z)
    (appendo x y z)))
```

17

```
(()
 (_0)
 (_0 _1)
 (_0 _1 _2)
 (_0 _1 _2 _3)
 (_0 _1 _2 _3 _4)).
```

What is the value of

```
(run 6 y
  (fresh (x z)
    (appendo x y z)))
```

18

```
(_0
 _0
 _0
 _0
 _0
 _0).
```

Since x is fresh, we know the first value comes from (*null*^{o} l), which succeeds, associating () with l, and then t, which is also fresh, is fused with *out*. But, how do we get the second through sixth values?

19 A new fresh variable *res* is passed into each recursion to *append*^{o}. After (*null*^{o} l) succeeds, t is fused with *res*, which is fresh, since *res* is passed as an argument (binding *out*) in the recursion.

What is the value of

```
(run 6 z
  (fresh (x y)
    (appendo x y z)))
```

20

```
(_0
 (_0 . _1)
 (_0 _1 . _2)
 (_0 _1 _2 . _3)
 (_0 _1 _2 _3 . _4)
 (_0 _1 _2 _3 _4 . _5)).
```

Now let's look at the first six values of x, y, and z at the same time.

What is the value of

```
(run 6 (x y z)
  (appendo x y z))
```

21

```
((() _0 _0)
 ((_0) _1 (_0 . _1))
 ((_0 _1) _2 (_0 _1 . _2))
 ((_0 _1 _2) _3 (_0 _1 _2 . _3))
 ((_0 _1 _2 _3) _4 (_0 _1 _2 _3 . _4))
 ((_0 _1 _2 _3 _4) _5 (_0 _1 _2 _3 _4 . _5))).
```

What value is associated with x in

```
(run* x
  (appendo
    '(cake)
    '(tastes yummy)
    x))
```

22 (cake tastes yummy).

What value is associated with x in

```
(run* x
  (fresh (y)
    (appendo
      `(cake & ice ,y)
      '(tastes yummy)
      x)))
```

23 (cake & ice _0 tastes yummy).

What value is associated with x in

```
(run* x
  (fresh (y)
    (appendo
      '(cake & ice cream)
      y
      x)))
```

24 (cake & ice cream . _0).

What value is associated with x in

```
(run 1 x
  (fresh (y)
    (appendo
      `(cake & ice . ,y)
      '(d t)
      x)))
```

25 (cake & ice d t),
because the successful (*null*^{o} y) associates the empty list with y.

What is the value of

```
(run 5 x
  (fresh (y)
    (appendo
      `(cake & ice . ,y)
      '(d t)
      x)))
```

26

```
((cake & ice d t)
 (cake & ice _0 d t)
 (cake & ice _0 _1 d t)
 (cake & ice _0 _1 _2 d t)
 (cake & ice _0 _1 _2 _3 d t)).
```

What is the value of

```
(run 5 y
  (fresh (x)
    (appendo
      `(cake & ice . ,y)
      '(d t)
      x)))
```

27

```
(()
 (_0)
 (_0 _1)
 (_0 _1 _2)
 (_0 _1 _2 _3)).
```

Let's plug in (_0 _1 _2) for *y* in

```
`(cake & ice . ,y).
```

Then we get

```
(cake & ice . (_0 _1 _2)).
```

What list is this the same as?

28

```
(cake & ice _0 _1 _2).
```

Right. Where have we seen the value of

```
(append '(cake & ice _0 _1 _2) '(d t))
```

29

This expression's value is the fourth list in frame 26.

What is the value of

```
(run 5 x
  (fresh (y)
    (appendᵒ
      `(cake & ice . ,y)
      `(d t . ,y)
      x)))
```

30

```
((cake & ice d t)
 (cake & ice _0 d t _0)
 (cake & ice _0 _1 d t _0 _1)
 (cake & ice _0 _1 _2 d t _0 _1 _2)
 (cake & ice _0 _1 _2 _3 d t _0 _1 _2 _3)).
```

What is the value of

```
(run* x
  (fresh (z)
    (appendᵒ
      '(cake & ice cream)
      `(d t . ,z)
      x)))
```

31

```
((cake & ice cream d t . _0)).
```

Why does the list contain only one value?

32

Because *t* does not change in the recursion. Therefore *z* stays fresh. The reason the list contains only one value is that (cake & ice cream) does not contain a variable, and is the only value considered in every **cond**^{e} line of *append*^{o}.

---

33 Let's try an example in which the first two arguments are variables.

What is the value of

```
(run 6 x
  (fresh (y)
    (appendᵒ x y '(cake & ice d t))))
```

```
(()
 (cake)
 (cake &)
 (cake & ice)
 (cake & ice d)
 (cake & ice d t)).
```

---

34 How might we describe these values?

The values include all of the prefixes of the list (cake & ice d t).

---

35 Now let's try this variation.

```
(run 6 y
  (fresh (x)
    (appendᵒ x y '(cake & ice d t))))
```

What is its value?

```
((cake & ice d t)
 (& ice d t)
 (ice d t)
 (d t)
 (t)
 ()).
```

---

36 How might we describe these values?

The values include all of the suffixes of the list (cake & ice d t).

---

37 Let's combine the previous two results.

What is the value of

```
(run 6 (x y)
  (appendᵒ x y '(cake & ice d t)))
```

```
((() (cake & ice d t))
 ((cake) (& ice d t))
 ((cake &) (ice d t))
 ((cake & ice) (d t))
 ((cake & ice d) (t))
 ((cake & ice d t) ())).
```

---

38 How might we describe these values?

Each value includes two lists that, when appended together, form the list

(cake & ice d t).

39 What is the value of

```
(run 7 (x y)
  (appendº x y '(cake & ice d t)))
```

This expression has no value, since *append*^{o} is still looking for the seventh value.

40 Would we prefer that this expression's value be that of frame 37?

Yes, that would make sense.

How can we change the definition of *append*^{o} so that these expressions have the same value?

† Thank you, Alain Colmerauer (1941–2017), and thanks, Carl Hewitt (1945–) and Philippe Roussel (1945–).

41 Swap the last two goals of *append*^{o}.

```
(defrel (appendº l t out)
  (condᵉ
    ((nullº l) (≡ t out))
    ((fresh (a d res)
       (consº a d l)
       (consº a res out)
       (appendº d t res)))))
```

42 Now, using this revised definition of *append*^{o}, what is the value of

```
(run* (x y)
  (appendº x y '(cake & ice d t)))
```

The same six values are in frame 37. This shows there are only six values.

The First Commandment

Within each sequence of goals, move non-recursive goals before recursive goals.

Define *swappend*^{o}, which is just *append*^{o} with its two **cond**^{e} lines swapped.

43 Here it is.

```
(defrel (swappendᵒ l t out)
  (condᵉ
    ((fresh (a d res)
       (consᵒ a d l)
       (consᵒ a res out)
       (swappendᵒ d t res)))
    ((nullᵒ l) (≡ t out))))
```

What is the value of

```
(run* (x y)
  (swappendᵒ x y '(cake & ice d t)))
```

44 The same six values as in frame 37.

The Law of Swapping cond^e Lines

Swapping two cond^e lines does not affect the values contributed by cond^e.

Consider this definition.

```
(define (unwrap x)
  (cond
    ((pair? x) (unwrap (car x)))
    (#t x)))
```

What is the value of

```
(unwrap '((((pizza)))))
```

45 pizza.

What is the value of

```
(unwrap '((((pizza pie) with)) garlic))
```

46 pizza.

Translate and simplify *unwrap*.

47 That's a slice of pizza!

```
(defrel (unwrapᵒ x out)
  (condᵉ
    ((fresh (a)
       (carᵒ x a)
       (unwrapᵒ a out)))
    ((≡ x out))))
```

What is the value of

```
(run* x
  (unwrapᵒ '(((pizza))) x))
```

48 ((((pizza)))
((pizza))
(pizza)
pizza).

The last value of the list seems right. In what way are the other values correct?

49 They represent partially wrapped versions of the list (((pizza))). And the first value is the fully-wrapped original list (((pizza))).†

† *unwrap*ᵒ is a tricky relation whose behavior does not fully comply with the behavior of the function *unwrap*. Nevertheless, by keeping track of the fusing, you can follow this pizza example.

DON'T PANIC

Thank you, Douglas Adams (1952–2001).

What value is associated with x in

```
(run 1 x
  (unwrapᵒ x 'pizza))
```

50 pizza.

What value is associated with x in (**run** 1 x (*unwrap*^{o} \`((,x)) 'pizza))	[51] pizza.
What is the value of (**run** 5 x (*unwrap*^{o} x 'pizza))	[52] (pizza (pizza . $\_0$) ((pizza . $\_0$) . $\_1$) (((pizza . $\_0$) . $\_1$) . $\_2$) ((((pizza . $\_0$) . $\_1$) . $\_2$) . $\_3$)).
What is the value of (**run** 5 x (*unwrap*^{o} x '((pizza))))	[53] (((pizza)) (((pizza)) . $\_0$) ((((pizza)) . $\_0$) . $\_1$) (((((pizza)) . $\_0$) . $\_1$) . $\_2$) ((((((pizza)) . $\_0$) . $\_1$) . $\_2$) . $\_3$)).
What is the value of (**run** 5 x (*unwrap*^{o} \`((,x)) 'pizza))	[54] (pizza (pizza . $\_0$) ((pizza . $\_0$) . $\_1$) (((pizza . $\_0$) . $\_1$) . $\_2$) ((((pizza . $\_0$) . $\_1$) . $\_2$) . $\_3$)).
This might be a good time for a pizza break.	[55] Good idea.

⟹ Now go get a pizza and put it in your mouth! ⟸

This space reserved for

PIZZA STAINS!

5.
Members Only

Consider this function.

```
(define (mem x l)
  (cond
    ((null? l) #f)
    ((equal? (car l) x) l)
    (#t (mem x (cdr l)))))
```

What is the value of

```
(mem 'fig
  '(roll okra fig beet roll pea))
```

1 (fig beet roll pea).

What is the value of

```
(mem 'fig
  '(roll okra beet beet roll pea))
```

2 #f.

What is the value of

```
(mem 'roll
  (mem 'fig
    '(roll okra fig beet roll pea)))
```

3 So familiar,

(roll pea).

Here is the translation of *mem*.

```
(defrel (memᵒ x l out)
  (condᵉ
    ((nullᵒ l) #u)
    ((fresh (a)
        (carᵒ l a)
        (≡ a x))
      (≡ l out))
    (#s
      (fresh (d)
        (cdrᵒ l d)
        (memᵒ x d out)))))
```

Do we know how to simplify mem^o

4 Of course, we can simplify it as in frame 3:47, by following **The Law of #u**, and by following **The Law of #s**.

```
(defrel (memᵒ x l out)
  (condᵉ
    ((carᵒ l x) (≡ l out))
    ((fresh (d)
        (cdrᵒ l d)
        (memᵒ x d out)))))
```

What is the value of

(**run*** *q*
  (*mem*^{o} 'fig '(pea) '(pea)))

5 ().
Since the *car* of (pea) is not fig, fig, (pea), and (pea) do not have the *mem*^{o} relationship.

What value is associated with *out* in

(**run*** *out*
  (*mem*^{o} 'fig '(fig) *out*))

6 (fig).
Since the *car* of (fig) is fig, fig, (fig), and (fig) have the *mem*^{o} relationship.

What value is associated with *out* in

(**run*** *out*
  (*mem*^{o} 'fig '(fig pea) *out*))

7 (fig pea).

What value is associated with *r* in

(**run*** *r*
  (*mem*^{o} *r*
    '(roll okra fig beet fig pea)
    '(fig beet fig pea)))

8 fig.

What is the value of

(**run*** *x*
  (*mem*^{o} 'fig '(fig pea) \`(pea ,*x*)))

9 (),
because there is no value that, when associated with *x*, makes \`(pea ,*x*) be (fig pea).

What value is associated with *x* in

(**run*** *x*
  (*mem*^{o} 'fig '(fig pea) \`(,*x* pea)))

10 fig,
when the value associated with *x* is fig, then \`(,*x* pea) is (fig pea).

What is the value of

(**run*** *out*
  (*mem*^{o} 'fig '(beet fig pea) *out*))

11 ((fig pea)).

12 In this **run** 1 expression, for any goal *g* how many times does *out* get an association?

(**run** 1 *out* *g*)

At most once, as we have seen in frame 3:13.

---

13 What is the value of

```
(run 1 out
  (memo 'fig '(fig fig pea) out))
```

((fig fig pea)).

---

14 What is the value of

```
(run* out
  (memo 'fig '(fig fig pea) out))
```

The same value, we expect.

---

15 No. The value is ((fig fig pea) (fig pea)).

This is quite a surprise.

---

16 Why is ((fig fig pea) (fig pea)) the value?

We know from **The Law of cond**^{e} that every successful **cond**^{e} line contributes one or more values. The first **cond**^{e} line succeeds and contributes the value (fig fig pea). The second **cond**^{e} line contains a recursion. This recursion succeeds, therefore the second **cond**^{e} line succeeds, contributing the value (fig pea).

---

17 In this respect the **cond** in *mem?* differs from the **cond**^{e} in *mem*^{o}.

We shall bear this difference in mind.

---

18 What is the value of

```
(run* out
  (fresh (x)
    (memo 'fig `(a ,x c fig e) out)))
```

((fig c fig e) (fig e)).

What is the value of

```
(run 5 (x y)
  (memº 'fig `(fig d fig e . ,y) x))
```

19
```
(((fig d fig e . _0) _0)
 ((fig e . _0) _0)
 ((fig . _0) (fig . _0))
 ((fig . _0) (_1 fig . _0))
 ((fig . _0) (_1 _2 fig . _0))).
```

Explain how *y*, reified as $\_0$, remains fresh in the first two values.

20 The first value corresponds to finding the first fig in that list, and the second value corresponds to finding the second fig in that list. In both cases, *mem*^{o} succeeds without associating a value to *y*.

Where do the other three values associated with *y* come from?

21 In order for

```
(memº 'fig `(fig d fig e . ,y) x)
```

to contribute values beyond those first two, there must be a fig in `(e . ,y), and therefore in *y*.

So *mem*^{o} is creating all the possible suffixes with fig as an element.

22 That's very interesting!

Remember *rember*.

```
(define (rember x l)
  (cond
    ((null? l) '())
    ((equal? (car l) x) (cdr l))
    (#t (cons (car l)
          (rember x (cdr l))))))
```

23 Of course, it's an old friend.

What is the value of

```
(rember 'pea '(a b pea d pea e))
```

24 (a b d pea e).

Here is the translation of *rember*.

```
(defrel (rembero x l out)
  (conde
    ((nullo l) (≡ '() out))
    ((fresh (a)
       (caro l a)
       (≡ a x))
     (cdro l out))
    (#s
     (fresh (res)
       (fresh (d)
         (cdro l d)
         (rembero x d res))
       (fresh (a)
         (caro l a)
         (conso a res out))))))
```

Do we know how to simplify *rember*^{o}

25 Yes, we can simplify *rember*^{o} as in frames 4:10 to 4:12, and by following **The Law of #s** and **The First Commandment**.

```
(defrel (rembero x l out)
  (conde
    ((nullo l) (≡ '() out))
    ((conso x out l))
    ((fresh (a d res)
       (conso a d l)
       (conso a res out)
       (rembero x d res)))))
```

What is the value of

```
(run* out
  (rembero 'pea '(pea) out))
```

26 (() (pea)).
When *l* is (pea), both the second and third **cond**^{e} lines in *rember*^{o} contribute values.

What is the value of

```
(run* out
  (rembero 'pea '(pea pea) out))
```

27 ((pea) (pea) (pea pea)).
When *l* is (pea pea), both the second and third **cond**^{e} lines in *rember*^{o} contribute values. The second **cond**^{e} line contributes the first value. The recursion in the third **cond**^{e} line contributes the two values in the frame above, () and (pea). The second *cons*^{o} relates the two contributed values in the recursion with the last two values of this expression, (pea) and (pea pea).

What is the value of

```
(run* out
  (fresh (y z)
    (rembero y `(a b ,y d ,z e) out)))
```

28 ((b a d _0 e)
 (a b d _0 e)
 (a b d _0 e)
 (a b d _0 e)
 (a b _0 d e)
 (a b e d _0)
 (a b _0 d _1 e)).

Why is

(b a d _0 e)

a value?

29 It looks like b and a have been swapped, and y has disappeared.

No. Why does b come first?

30 The b is first because the a has been removed from the *car*.

Why does the list contain a now?

31 In order to remove a, a is associated with y. The value of the y in the list is a.

What is _0 in this list?

32 The reified variable z. In this value z remains fresh.

Why is

(a b d _0 e)

the second value?

33 It looks like y has disappeared.

No. Has the b in the original list been removed?

34 Yes.

Why does the list still contain a b

35 In order to remove b from the list, b is associated with y. The value of the y in the list is b.

Why is

(a b d $\_{0}$ e)

the third value?

36 Is it for the same reason that (a b d $\_{0}$ e) is the second value?

Not quite. Has the b in the original list been removed?

37 No,
but the y has been removed.

Why is

(a b d $\_{0}$ e)

the fourth value?

38 Because the d has been removed from the list.

Why does this list still contain a d

39 In order to remove d from the list, d is associated with y.

Why is

(a b $\_{0}$ d e)

the fifth value?

40 Because the z has been removed from the list.

Why does this list contain $\_{0}$

41 In order to remove z from the list, z is fused with y. These variables remain fresh, and the y in the list is reified as $\_{0}$.

Why is

(a b e d $\_{0}$)

the sixth value?

42 Because the e has been removed from the list.

Why does this list still contain an e

43 In order to remove e from the list, e is associated with y.

What variable does the $\_{0}$ contained in this list represent?

44 The reified variable z. In this value z remains fresh.

---

z and y are fused in the fifth value, but not in sixth value.

45 Correct.

cond^{e} lines contribute values independently of one another. The case that removes z from the list (and fuses it with y) is independent of the case that removes e from the list (and associates e with y).

Very well stated. Why is

(a b $\_{0}$ d $\_{1}$ e)

the seventh value?

46 Because we have not removed anything from the list.

Why does this list contain $\_{0}$ and $\_{1}$

47 These are the reified variables y and z. This case is independent of the previous cases. Here, y and z remain different fresh variables.

What is the value of

```
(run* (y z)
  (rembero y `(,y d ,z e) `(,y d e)))
```

48

```
((d d)
 (d d)
 (_0 _0)
 (e e)).
```

Why is

(d d)

the first value?

49 When y is d and z is d, then

(*rember*^{o} 'd '(d d d e) '(d d e))

succeeds.

Why is

(d d)

the second value?

50 When y is d and z is d, then

(*rember*^{o} 'd '(d d d e) '(d d e))

succeeds.

Why is

$(\_0\ \_0)$

the third value?

51 *y* and *z* are fused, but they remain fresh.

How is

(d d)

the first value?

52 *rember^o* removes *y* from the list \`(,*y* d ,*z* e), yielding the list \`(d ,*z* e); \`(d ,*z* e) is the same as the third argument to *rember$^o$*, \`(,*y* d e), only when d is associated with both *y* and *z*.

How is

(d d)

the second value?

53 Next, *rember^o* removes d from the list \`(,*y* d ,*z* e), yielding the list \`(,*y* ,*z* e); \`(,*y* ,*z* e) is the same as the third argument to *rember$^o$*, \`(,*y* d e), only when d is associated with *z*. Also, in order to remove d, d is associated with *y*.

How is

$(\_0\ \_0)$

the third value?

54 Next, *rember^o* removes *z* from the list \`(,*y* d ,*z* e), yielding the list \`(,*y* d e); \`(,*y* d e) is always the same as the third argument to *rember$^o$*, \`(,*y* d e). Also, in order to remove *z*, *y* is fused with *z*.

Finally, how is

(e e)

the fourth value?

55 *rember^o* removes e from the list \`(,*y* d ,*z* e), yielding the list \`(,*y* d ,*z*); \`(,*y* d ,*z*) is the same as the third argument to *rember$^o$*, \`(,*y* d e), only when e is associated with *z*. Also, in order to remove e, e is associated with *y*.

What is the value of

(run 4 (*y z w out*)
  (*rember^o y* \`(,*z* . ,*w*) *out*))

56 $((\_0\ \_0\ \_1\ \_1)$
$(\_0\ \_1\ ()\ (\_1))$
$(\_0\ \_1\ (\_0 \cdot \_2)\ (\_1 \cdot \_2))$
$(\_0\ \_1\ (\_2)\ (\_1\ \_2)))$.

How is

$(\_{0}\ \_{0}\ \_{1}\ \_{1})$

the first value?

57 For the first value, *rember*^{o} removes z from the list `` `(,z . ,w) ``. *rember*^{o} fuses y with z and fuses w with *out*.

How is

$(\_{0}\ \_{1}\ ()\ (\_{1}))$

the second value?

58 *rember*^{o} removes no value from the list `` `(,z . ,w) ``. (*null*^{o} *l*) in the first **cond**^{e} line then succeeds, associating w with the empty list.

How is

$(\_{0}\ \_{1}\ (\_{0}\ .\ \_{2})\ (\_{1}\ .\ \_{2}))$

the third value?

59 *rember*^{o} removes no value from the list `` `(,z . ,w) ``. The second **cond**^{e} line also succeeds, and associates the pair `` `(,y . ,out) `` with w. The *out* of the recursion, however, is just the fresh variable *res*, and the last *cons*^{o} in *rember*^{o} associates the pair `` `(,z . ,res) `` with *out*.

How is

$(\_{0}\ \_{1}\ (\_{2})\ (\_{1}\ \_{2}))$

the fourth value?

60 This is the same as the second value, $(\_{0}\ \_{1}\ ()\ (\_{1}))$, except with an additional recursion.

If we had instead written

(**run** 5 (*y z w out*)
  (*rember*^{o} *y* `` `(,z . ,w) `` *out*))

what would be the fifth value?

61 $(\_{0}\ \_{1}\ (\_{2}\ \_{0}\ .\ \_{3})\ (\_{1}\ \_{2}\ .\ \_{3}))$, because this is the same as the third value, $(\_{0}\ \_{1}\ (\_{0}\ .\ \_{2})\ (\_{1}\ .\ \_{2}))$, except with an additional recursion.

$\Longrightarrow$ Now go munch on some carrots. $\Longleftarrow$

This space reserved for

CARROT STAINS!

6.
The Fun Never Ends...

Here is a useful definition.

```
(defrel (alwayso)
  (conde
    (#s)
    ((alwayso))))
```

What value is associated with q in

```
(run 1 q
  (alwayso))
```

1 $\_0$.

What is the value of

```
(run 1 q
  (conde
    (#s)
    ((alwayso))))
```

2 $(\_0)$,
because the first **cond**^{e} line succeeds.

Compare (*always*^{o}) to **#s**.

3 (*always*^{o}) succeeds any number of times, whereas **#s** succeeds only once.

What is the value of

```
(run* q
  (alwayso))
```

4 It has no value,
since **run*** never finishes building the list $(\_0\ \_0\ \_0\ \cdots$

What is the value of

```
(run* q
  (conde
    (#s)
    ((alwayso))))
```

5 It has no value,
since **run*** never finishes building the list $(\_0\ \_0\ \_0\ \cdots$

What is the value of

```
(run 5 q
  (alwayso))
```

6 $(\_0\ \_0\ \_0\ \_0\ \_0)$.

And what is the value of

```
(run 5 q
  (≡ 'onion q)
  (alwayso))
```

7 (onion onion onion onion onion).

What is the value of

```
(run 1 q
  (alwayso)
  #u)
```

8 It has no value,
because (*always*^{o}) succeeds, followed by #u, which causes (*always*^{o}) to be retried, which succeeds again, which leads to #u again, etc.

What is the value of

```
(run 1 q
  (≡ 'garlic q)
  #s
  (≡ 'onion q))
```

9 ().

What is the value of

```
(run 1 q
  (≡ 'garlic q)
  (alwayso)
  (≡ 'onion q))
```

10 It has no value.
First garlic is associated with q, then *always*^{o} succeeds, then (≡ 'onion q) fails, since q is already garlic. This causes (*always*^{o}) to be retried, which succeeds again, which leads to (≡ 'onion q) failing again, etc.

What is the value of

```
(run 1 q
  (conde
    ((≡ 'garlic q) (alwayso))
    ((≡ 'onion q)))
  (≡ 'onion q))
```

11 (onion).

What happens if we try for more values?

```
(run 2 q
  (condᵉ
    ((≡ 'garlic q) (alwaysᵒ))
    ((≡ 'onion q)))
  (≡ 'onion q))
```

12 It has no value, since only the second **cond**^{e} line associates onion with q.

So does this give more values?

```
(run 5 q
  (condᵉ
    ((≡ 'garlic q) (alwaysᵒ))
    ((≡ 'onion q) (alwaysᵒ)))
  (≡ 'onion q))
```

13 Yes, it yields as many as are requested,

(onion onion onion onion onion).

The (*always*^{o}) in the first **cond**^{e} line succeeds five times, but contributes none of the five values, since then garlic would be in the list.

Here is an unusual definition.

```
(defrel (neverᵒ)
  (neverᵒ))
```

Is (*never*^{o}) a goal?

14 Yes it is!

Compare #u to (*never*^{o}).

15 #u is a goal that fails, whereas (*never*^{o}) is a goal that neither succeeds nor fails.

What is the value of

```
(run 1 q
  (neverᵒ))
```

16 This **run** 1 expression has no value.

What is the value of

```
(run 1 q
  #u
  (neverᵒ))
```

17 (), because #u fails before (*never*^{o}) is attempted.

What is the value of

```
(run 1 q
  (conde
    (#s)
    ((nevero))))
```

18 $(\_{0})$,
because the first **cond**^{e} line succeeds.

What is the value of

```
(run 1 q
  (conde
    ((nevero))
    (#s)))
```

19 $(\_{0})$,
because **The Law of Swapping cond^e Lines** says the expressions in this and the previous frame have the same values.

What is the value of

```
(run 2 q
  (conde
    (#s)
    ((nevero))))
```

20 It has no value,
because **run*** never finishes determining the *second* value; the goal (*never*^{o}) never succeeds and never fails.

What is the value of

```
(run 1 q
  (conde
    (#s)
    ((nevero)))
  #u)
```

21 It has no value.
After the first **cond**^{e} line succeeds, #u fails. This causes (*never*^{o}) in the second **cond**^{e} line to be tried; as we have seen, (*never*^{o}) neither succeeds nor fails.

What is the value of

```
(run 5 q
  (conde
    ((nevero))
    ((alwayso))
    ((nevero))))
```

22 It is $(\_{0}\ \_{0}\ \_{0}\ \_{0}\ \_{0})$.

What is the value of

```
(run 6 q
  (conde
    ((≡ 'spicy q) (nevero))
    ((≡ 'hot q) (nevero))
    ((≡ 'apple q) (alwayso))
    ((≡ 'cider q) (alwayso))))
```

23 It is (apple cider apple cider apple cider). As we know from frame 1:61, the order of the values does *not* matter.

Can we use *never*^{o} and *always*^{o} in other recursive definitions?

24 Yes.

Here is the definition of *very-recursive*^{o}.

```
(defrel (very-recursiveo)
  (conde
    ((nevero))
    ((very-recursiveo))
    ((alwayso))
    ((very-recursiveo))
    ((nevero))))
```

Does (**run** 1000000 *q* (*very-recursive*^{o})) have a value?

25 Yes, indeed! A list of one million $\_{0}$ values.

⟹ Take a peek "Under the Hood" at chapter 10. ⟸

7.
A Bit Too Much

Is 0 a *bit*?

1 Yes.

Is 1 a bit?

2 Yes.

Is 2 a bit?

3 No.
A bit is either a 0 or a 1.

Which bits are represented by a fresh variable x

4 0 and 1.

Here is *bit-xor*^{o}.

```
(defrel (bit-xor^o x y r)
  (cond^e
    ((≡ 0 x) (≡ 0 y) (≡ 0 r))
    ((≡ 0 x) (≡ 1 y) (≡ 1 r))
    ((≡ 1 x) (≡ 0 y) (≡ 1 r))
    ((≡ 1 x) (≡ 1 y) (≡ 0 r))))
```

When is 0 the value of r

5 When x and y have the same value.†

† Another way to define *bit-xor*^{o} is to use *bit-nand*^{o}

```
(defrel (bit-xor^o x y r)
  (fresh (s t u)
    (bit-nand^o x y s)
    (bit-nand^o s y u)
    (bit-nand^o x s t)
    (bit-nand^o t u r))),
```

where *bit-nand*^{o} is

```
(defrel (bit-nand^o x y r)
  (cond^e
    ((≡ 0 x) (≡ 0 y) (≡ 1 r))
    ((≡ 0 x) (≡ 1 y) (≡ 1 r))
    ((≡ 1 x) (≡ 0 y) (≡ 1 r))
    ((≡ 1 x) (≡ 1 y) (≡ 0 r)))).
```

Both *bit-xor*^{o} and *bit-nand*^{o} are universal binary Boolean relations, since either can be used to define all other binary Boolean relations.

Demonstrate this using **run***.

6

```
(run* (x y)
  (bit-xor^o x y 0))
```

which has the value

```
((0 0)
 (1 1)).
```

When is 1 the value of r

7 When x and y have different values.

Demonstrate this using **run***.

8
```
(run* (x y)
  (bit-xor^o x y 1))
```
which has the value
```
((0 1)
 (1 0)).
```

What is the value of
```
(run* (x y r)
  (bit-xor^o x y r))
```

9
```
((0 0 0)
 (0 1 1)
 (1 0 1)
 (1 1 0)).
```

Here is *bit-and*^{o}.

```
(defrel (bit-and^o x y r)
  (cond^e
    ((≡ 0 x) (≡ 0 y) (≡ 0 r))
    ((≡ 1 x) (≡ 0 y) (≡ 0 r))
    ((≡ 0 x) (≡ 1 y) (≡ 0 r))
    ((≡ 1 x) (≡ 1 y) (≡ 1 r))))
```

When is 1 the value of r

10 When x and y are both 1.†

† Another way to define *bit-and*^{o} is to use *bit-nand*^{o} and *bit-not*^{o}

```
(defrel (bit-and^o x y r)
  (fresh (s)
    (bit-nand^o x y s)
    (bit-not^o s r)))
```

where *bit-not*^{o} itself is defined in terms of *bit-nand*^{o}

```
(defrel (bit-not^o x r)
  (bit-nand^o x x r)).
```

Demonstrate this using **run***.

11
```
(run* (x y)
  (bit-and^o x y 1))
```
which has the value
```
((1 1)).
```

Here is *half-adder*^{o}.

```
(defrel (half-adderᵒ x y r c)
  (bit-xorᵒ x y r)
  (bit-andᵒ x y c))
```

What value is associated with r in

```
(run* r
  (half-adderᵒ 1 1 r 1))
```

12 0.†

† *half-adder*^{o} can be redefined,

```
(defrel (half-adderᵒ x y r c)
  (condᵉ
    ((≡ 0 x) (≡ 0 y) (≡ 0 r) (≡ 0 c))
    ((≡ 1 x) (≡ 0 y) (≡ 1 r) (≡ 0 c))
    ((≡ 0 x) (≡ 1 y) (≡ 1 r) (≡ 0 c))
    ((≡ 1 x) (≡ 1 y) (≡ 0 r) (≡ 1 c)))).
```

What is the value of

```
(run* (x y r c)
  (half-adderᵒ x y r c))
```

13 ((0 0 0 0)
(0 1 1 0)
(1 0 1 0)
(1 1 0 1)).

Describe *half-adder*^{o}.

14 Given the bits x, y, r, and c, *half-adder*^{o} satisfies $x + y = r + 2 \cdot c$.

Here is *full-adder*^{o}.

```
(defrel (full-adderᵒ b x y r c)
  (fresh (w xy wz)
    (half-adderᵒ x y w xy)
    (half-adderᵒ w b r wz)
    (bit-xorᵒ xy wz c)))
```

The x, y, r, and c variables serve the same purpose as in *half-adder*^{o}. *full-adder*^{o} also expects a carry-in bit, b. What values are associated with r and c in

```
(run* (r c)
  (full-adderᵒ 0 1 1 r c))
```

15 (0 1).†

† *full-adder*^{o} can be redefined,

```
(defrel (full-adderᵒ b x y r c)
  (condᵉ
    ((≡ 0 b) (≡ 0 x) (≡ 0 y) (≡ 0 r) (≡ 0 c))
    ((≡ 1 b) (≡ 0 x) (≡ 0 y) (≡ 1 r) (≡ 0 c))
    ((≡ 0 b) (≡ 1 x) (≡ 0 y) (≡ 1 r) (≡ 0 c))
    ((≡ 1 b) (≡ 1 x) (≡ 0 y) (≡ 0 r) (≡ 1 c))
    ((≡ 0 b) (≡ 0 x) (≡ 1 y) (≡ 1 r) (≡ 0 c))
    ((≡ 1 b) (≡ 0 x) (≡ 1 y) (≡ 0 r) (≡ 1 c))
    ((≡ 0 b) (≡ 1 x) (≡ 1 y) (≡ 0 r) (≡ 1 c))
    ((≡ 1 b) (≡ 1 x) (≡ 1 y) (≡ 1 r) (≡ 1 c)))).
```

What value is associated with $(r\ c)$ in

(**run*** $(r\ c)$
  (*full-adder*^{o} 1 1 1 r c))

[16] (1 1).

What is the value of

(**run*** $(b\ x\ y\ r\ c)$
  (*full-adder*^{o} b x y r c))

[17] ((0 0 0 0 0)
(1 0 0 1 0)
(0 1 0 1 0)
(1 1 0 0 1)
(0 0 1 1 0)
(1 0 1 0 1)
(0 1 1 0 1)
(1 1 1 1 1)).

Describe *full-adder*^{o}.

[18] Given the bits b, x, y, r, and c, *full-adder*^{o} satisfies $b + x + y = r + 2 \cdot c$.

What is a *natural number*?

[19] A natural number is an integer greater than or equal to zero. Are there any other kinds of numbers?

Is each number represented by a bit?

[20] No.
Each number is represented as a *list* of bits.

Which list represents the number zero?

[21] The empty list ()?

Correct. Good guess.

[22] Does (0) also represent the number zero?

No.

Each number has a unique representation, therefore (0) cannot also be zero. Furthermore, (0) does not represent a number.

Which list represents $1 \cdot 2^0$? That is to say, which list represents the number one?

23 (1).

Which number is represented by

(1 0 1)

24 5,

because the value of (1 0 1) is $1 \cdot 2^0 + 0 \cdot 2^1 + 1 \cdot 2^2$, which is the same as $1 + 0 + 4$, which is five.

Correct. Which number is represented by

(1 1 1)

25 7,

because the value of (1 1 1) is $1 \cdot 2^0 + 1 \cdot 2^1 + 1 \cdot 2^2$, which is the same as $1 + 2 + 4$, which is seven.

Also correct. Which list represents 9?

26 (1 0 0 1),

because the value of (1 0 0 1) is $1 \cdot 2^0 + 0 \cdot 2^1 + 0 \cdot 2^2 + 1 \cdot 2^3$, which is the same as $1+0+0+8$, which is nine.

Yes. How do we represent 6?

27 As the list (1 1 0)?

No. Try again.

28 Then it must be (0 1 1),

because the value of (0 1 1) is $0 \cdot 2^0 + 1 \cdot 2^1 + 1 \cdot 2^2$, which is the same as $0 + 2 + 4$, which is six.

Correct. Does this seem unusual?

29 Yes, it seems very unusual.

How do we represent 19?

30 As the list (1 1 0 0 1)?

Yes. How do we represent 1729?

31 As the list (1 0 0 0 0 0 1 1 0 1 1)?

Correct again. What is interesting about the lists that represent the numbers we have seen?

32 They contain only 0's and 1's.

Yes. What else is interesting?

33 Every non-empty list ends with a 1.

Does every list representation of a number end with a 1?

34 Almost always, except for the empty list, (), which represents zero.

Compare the numbers represented by *n* and `(0 • ,*n*).

35 `(0 • ,*n*) is twice *n*.
But *n* cannot be (), since `(0 • ,*n*) is (0), which does not represent a number.

If *n* is (1 0 1), what is `(0 • ,*n*)

36 (0 1 0 1),
since twice five is ten.

Compare the numbers represented by *n* and `(1 • ,*n*)

37 `(1 • ,*n*) is one more than twice *n*,
even when *n* is ().

If *n* is (1 0 1), what is `(1 • ,*n*)

38 (1 1 0 1),
since one more than twice five is eleven.

---

39 What is the value of
(*build-num* 0)

().

40 What is the value of
(*build-num* 36)

(0 0 1 0 0 1).

41 What is the value of
(*build-num* 19)

(1 1 0 0 1).

42 Define *build-num*.

Here is one way to define it.

```
(define (build-num n)
  (cond
    ((zero? n) '())
    ((even? n)
     (cons 0
       (build-num (÷ n 2))))
    ((odd? n)
     (cons 1
       (build-num (÷ (− n 1) 2))))))
```

43 Redefine *build-num*, where (*zero?* *n*) is the question of the last **cond** line.

Here it is.

```
(define (build-num n)
  (cond
    ((odd? n)
     (cons 1
       (build-num (÷ (− n 1) 2))))
    ((and (not (zero? n)) (even? n))
     (cons 0
       (build-num (÷ n 2))))
    ((zero? n) '())))
```

Is there anything interesting about the previous definition of *build-num*

44 For any number n, one and only one **cond** question is true.

Can we rearrange these **cond** lines in any order?

45 Yes.

This is called the *non-overlapping property.*† It appears rather frequently throughout this and the next chapter.

† Thank you Edsger W. Dijkstra (1930–2002).

What is the sum of (1) and (1)

46 (0 1), which is two.

What is the sum of (0 0 0 1) and (1 1 1)

47 (1 1 1 1), which is fifteen.

What is the sum of (1 1 1) and (0 0 0 1)

48 This is also (1 1 1 1), which is fifteen.

What is the sum of (1 1 0 0 1) and ()

49 (1 1 0 0 1), which is nineteen.

What is the sum of () and (1 1 0 0 1)

50 This is also (1 1 0 0 1), which is nineteen.

What is the sum of (1 1 1 0 1) and (1)

51 (0 0 0 1 1), which is twenty-four.

Which number is represented by

`(,x 1)

52 It depends on what x is.

Which number would be represented by

`(,x 1)

if x were 0?

53 Two,
which is represented by (0 1).

Which number would be represented by

`(,x 1)

if x were 1?

54 Three,
which is represented by (1 1).

So which numbers are represented by

`(,x 1)

55 Two and three.

Which numbers are represented by

`(,x ,x 1)

56 Four and seven,
which are represented by (0 0 1) and (1 1 1), respectively.

Which numbers are represented by

`(,x 0 ,y 1)

57 Eight, nine, twelve, and thirteen,
which are represented by (0 0 0 1), (1 0 0 1), (0 0 1 1), and (1 0 1 1), respectively.

Which numbers are represented by

`(,x 0 ,y ,z)

58 Once again, eight, nine, twelve, and thirteen,
which are represented by (0 0 0 1), (1 0 0 1), (0 0 1 1), and (1 0 1 1), respectively.

Which number is represented by

`(,x)

59 One,
which is represented by (1). Since (0) does not represent a number, x must be 1.

Which number is represented by

`(0 ,x)

60 Two,
which is represented by (0 1). Since (0 0) does not represent a number, x must be 1.

Which numbers are represented by

`(1 • ,z)

61 It depends on what z is. What does z represent?

Which number is represented by

`(1 • ,z)

where z is ()

62 One,
since (1 • ()) is (1).

Which number is represented by

`(1 • ,z)

where z is (1)

63 Three,
since (1 • (1)) is (1 1).

Which number is represented by

`(1 • ,z)

where z is (0 1)

64 Five,
since (1 • (0 1)) is (1 0 1).

So which numbers are represented by

`(1 • ,z)

65 All the odd numbers?

Right. Then, which numbers are represented by

`(0 • ,z)

66 All the even numbers?

Not quite. Which even number is not of the form `'(0 • ,z)`	67	Zero, which is represented by ().
For which values of z does `'(0 • ,z)` represent a number?	68	It represents a number for all z greater than zero.
Which numbers are represented by `'(0 0 • ,z)`	69	Every other even number, starting with four.
Which numbers are represented by `'(0 1 • ,z)`	70	Every other even number, starting with two.
Which numbers are represented by `'(1 0 • ,z)`	71	Every other odd number, starting with five.
Which numbers are represented by `'(1 0 ,y • ,z)`	72	Once again, every other odd number, starting with five.
Why do `'(1 0 • ,z)` and `'(1 0 ,y • ,z)` represent the same numbers?	73	Because z cannot be the empty list in `'(1 0 • ,z)` and y cannot be 0 when z is the empty list in `'(1 0 ,y • ,z)`.
Which numbers are represented by `'(0 ,y • ,z)`	74	Every even number, starting with two.
Which numbers are represented by `'(1 ,y • ,z)`	75	Every odd number, starting with three.

Which numbers are represented by

`(,y • ,z)

76 Every number, starting with one—in other words, the positive numbers.

Here is *pos*ᵒ.

```
(defrel (pos° n)
  (fresh (a d)
    (≡ `(,a • ,d) n)))
```

What value is associated with *q* in

```
(run* q
  (pos° '(0 1 1)))
```

77 $_{-0}$.

What value is associated with *q* in

```
(run* q
  (pos° '(1)))
```

78 $_{-0}$.

What is the value of

```
(run* q
  (pos° '()))
```

79 ().

What value is associated with *r* in

```
(run* r
  (pos° r))
```

80 ($_{-0}$ • $_{-1}$).

Does this mean that (*pos*ᵒ *r*) always succeeds when *r* is fresh?

81 Yes.

Which numbers are represented by

`(,x ,y • ,z)

82 Every number, starting with two—in other words, every number greater than one.

Here is $>1^o$. | 83 $\_{0}$.

```
(defrel (>1° n)
  (fresh (a ad dd)†
    (≡ `(,a ,ad . ,dd) n)))
```

What value is associated with q in

```
(run* q
  (>1° '(0 1 1)))
```

† The names *a*, *ad*, and *dd* correspond to *car*, *cadr*, and *cddr*. *cadr* is a Scheme function that stands for the *car* of the *cdr*, and *cddr* stands for the *cdr* of the *cdr*.

What is the value of

```
(run* q
  (>1° '(0 1)))
```

84 $(\_{0})$.

What is the value of

```
(run* q
  (>1° '(1)))
```

85 ().

What is the value of

```
(run* q
  (>1° '()))
```

86 ().

What value is associated with r in

```
(run* r
  (>1° r))
```

87 $(\_{0}\ \_{1}\ .\ \_{2})$.

Does this mean that $(>1^o\ r)$ always succeeds when r is fresh?

88 Yes.

What is the value of

```
(run 3 (x y r)
  (addero 0 x y r))
```

89 We have not seen *adder*^{o}. We understand, however, that (*adder*^{o} b n m r) satisfies the equation $b + n + m = r$, where b is a bit, and n, m, and r are numbers.

We find *adder*^{o}'s definition in frame 104. What is the value of

```
(run 3 (x y r)
  (addero 0 x y r))
```

90 $((\_{0}\ ()\ \_{0})$
$(()\ (\_{0}\ .\ \_{1})\ (\_{0}\ .\ \_{1}))$
$((1)\ (1)\ (0\ 1)))$.

(*adder*^{o} 0 x y r) sums x and y to produce r. For example, in the first value, a number added to zero is that number. In the second value, the sum of () and $(\_{0}\ .\ \_{1})$ is $(\_{0}\ .\ \_{1})$. In other words, the sum of zero and a positive number is the positive number.

Does ((1) (1) (0 1)) represent a *ground* value?

91 Yes.

Does $(\_{0}\ ()\ \_{0})$ represent a ground value?

92 No,
because it contains reified variables.

What can we say about the three values in frame 90?

93 The third value is ground, and the first two values are not.

Before reading the next frame,

Treat Yourself to a Hot Fudge Sundae!

What is the value of

```
(run 19 (x y r)
  (addero 0 x y r))
```

94

```
((_0 () _0)
 (() (_0 . _1) (_0 . _1))
 ((1) (1) (0 1))
 ((1) (0 _0 . _1) (1 _0 . _1))
 ((1) (1 1) (0 0 1))
 ((0 1) (0 1) (0 0 1))
 ((1) (1 0 _0 . _1) (0 1 _0 . _1))
 ((0 _0 . _1) (1) (1 _0 . _1))
 ((1) (1 1 1) (0 0 0 1))
 ((1 1) (0 1) (1 0 1))
 ((1 1) (1) (0 0 1))
 ((1) (1 1 0 _0 . _1) (0 0 1 _0 . _1))
 ((1) (1 1 1 1) (0 0 0 0 1))
 ((1) (1 1 1 0 _0 . _1) (0 0 0 1 _0 . _1))
 ((1 0 _0 . _1) (1) (0 1 _0 . _1))
 ((1) (1 1 1 1 1) (0 0 0 0 0 1))
 ((0 1) (1 1) (1 0 1))
 ((1 1 1) (1) (0 0 0 1))
 ((1 1) (1 1) (0 1 1))).
```

How many of its values are ground and how many are not?

95 Eleven are ground and eight are not.

What are the nonground values?

96

```
((_0 () _0)
 (() (_0 . _1) (_0 . _1))
 ((1) (0 _0 . _1) (1 _0 . _1))
 ((1) (1 0 _0 . _1) (0 1 _0 . _1))
 ((0 _0 . _1) (1) (1 _0 . _1))
 ((1) (1 1 0 _0 . _1) (0 0 1 _0 . _1))
 ((1) (1 1 1 0 _0 . _1) (0 0 0 1 _0 . _1))
 ((1 0 _0 . _1) (1) (0 1 _0 . _1))).
```

What is an interesting property that these nonground values possess?

97 Variables appear in r, and in either x or y, but not in both.

98 Describe the third nonground value.

Here x is (1) and y is (0 _0 . _1), a positive even number. Adding x to y yields all but the first odd number.

Is the third nonground value the same as the fifth nonground value?

---

99 Almost,
since $x + y = y + x$.

Oh.

---

100 Does each nonground value have a corresponding nonground value in which x and y are swapped?

No.
For example, the first two nonground values do not correspond to any other values.

---

101 Describe the fourth nonground value.

Frame 72 shows that (1 0 _0 . _1) represents every other odd number, starting at five. Adding one to the fourth nonground number produces every other even number, starting at six, which is represented by (0 1 _0 . _1).

---

102 What are the ground values of frame 94?

```
(((1) (1) (0 1))
 ((1) (1 1) (0 0 1))
 ((0 1) (0 1) (0 0 1))
 ((1) (1 1 1) (0 0 0 1))
 ((1 1) (0 1) (1 0 1))
 ((1 1) (1) (0 0 1))
 ((1) (1 1 1 1) (0 0 0 0 1))
 ((1) (1 1 1 1 1) (0 0 0 0 0 1))
 ((0 1) (1 1) (1 0 1))
 ((1 1 1) (1) (0 0 0 1))
 ((1 1) (1 1) (0 1 1))).
```

---

103 What is another interesting property of these ground values?

Each list cannot be created from any list in frame 96, regardless of which values are chosen for the variables there. This is an example of the non-overlapping property described in frame 45.

⟹ First-time readers may skip to frame 114. ⟸

104 Here are *adder*^{o} and *gen-adder*^{o}.

```
(defrel (addero b n m r)
  (conde
    ((≡ 0 b) (≡ '() m) (≡ n r))
    ((≡ 0 b) (≡ '() n) (≡ m r)
     (poso m))
    ((≡ 1 b) (≡ '() m)
     (addero 0 n '(1) r))
    ((≡ 1 b) (≡ '() n) (poso m)
     (addero 0 '(1) m r))
    ((≡ '(1) n) (≡ '(1) m)
     (fresh (a c)
       (≡ `(,a ,c) r)
       (full-addero b 1 1 a c)))
    ((≡ '(1) n) (gen-addero b n m r))
    ((≡ '(1) m) (>1o n) (>1o r)
     (addero b '(1) n r))
    ((>1o n) (gen-addero b n m r))))
```

```
(defrel (gen-addero b n m r)
  (fresh (a c d e x y z)
    (≡ `(,a . ,x) n)
    (≡ `(,d . ,y) m) (poso y)
    (≡ `(,c . ,z) r) (poso z)
    (full-addero b a d c e)
    (addero e x y z)))
```

What is *b*

A *carry* bit.

What are n, m, and r	105	They are numbers.
What value is associated with s in (**run*** s (*gen-adder*^{o} 1 '(0 1 1) '(1 1) s))	106	(0 1 0 1).
What are a, c, d, and e	107	They are bits.
What are x, y, and z	108	They are numbers.
In the definition of *gen-adder*^{o}, (*pos*^{o} y) and (*pos*^{o} z) follow (≡ \`(,$d$ . ,$y$) $m$) and (≡ \`(,c . ,z) r), respectively. Why isn't there a (*pos*^{o} x)	109	Because in the first use of *gen-adder*^{o} from *adder*^{o}, n can be (1).
What about the other use of *gen-adder*^{o} from *adder*^{o}	110	(>**1**^{o} n) that precedes the use of *gen-adder*^{o} would be the same as if we had placed a (*pos*^{o} x) following (≡ \`(,a . ,x) n). But if we were to use (*pos*^{o} x) in *gen-adder*^{o}, then it would fail for n being (1).
Describe *gen-adder*^{o}.	111	Given the carry bit b, and the numbers n, m, and r, *gen-adder*^{o} satisfies $b+n+m=r$, provided that n is positive and m and r are greater than one.
What is the value of (**run*** (x y) (*adder*^{o} 0 x y '(1 0 1)))	112	(((1 0 1) ()) (() (1 0 1)) ((1) (0 0 1)) ((0 0 1) (1)) ((1 1) (0 1)) ((0 1) (1 1))).

113 Describe the values produced by

```
(run* (x y)
  (adder^o 0 x y '(1 0 1)))
```

The values are the pairs of numbers that sum to five.

---

114 We can define $+^o$ using $adder^o$.

```
(defrel (+^o n m k)
  (adder^o 0 n m k))
```

Use $+^o$ to generate the pairs of numbers that sum to five.

Here is an expression that generates the pairs of numbers that sum to five,

```
(run* (x y)
  (+^o x y '(1 0 1))).
```

---

115 What is the value of

```
(run* (x y)
  (+^o x y '(1 0 1)))
```

```
(((1 0 1) ())
 (() (1 0 1))
 ((1) (0 0 1))
 ((0 0 1) (1))
 ((1 1) (0 1))
 ((0 1) (1 1))).
```

---

116 Now define $-^o$ using $+^o$.

Wow.

```
(defrel (-^o n m k)
  (+^o m k n))
```

---

117 What is the value of

```
(run* q
  (-^o '(0 0 0 1) '(1 0 1) q))
```

((1 1)).

---

118 What is the value of

```
(run* q
  (-^o '(0 1 1) '(0 1 1) q))
```

(()).

119

What is the value of

```
(run* q
  (-o '(0 1 1) '(0 0 0 1) q))
```

().
Eight cannot be subtracted from six, since we do not represent negative numbers.

120

Here is *length*.

```
(define (length l)
  (cond
    ((null? l) 0)
    (#t (+ 1 (length (cdr l))))))
```

Define *length*^{o}.

That's familiar enough.

```
(defrel (lengtho l n)
  (conde
    ((nullo l) (≡ '() n))
    ((fresh (d res)
       (cdro l d)
       (+o '(1) res n)
       (lengtho d res)))))
```

121

What value is associated with n in

```
(run 1 n
  (lengtho '(jicama rhubarb guava) n))
```

(1 1).

122

And what value is associated with *ls* in

```
(run* ls
  (lengtho ls '(1 0 1)))
```

(_0 _1 _2 _3 _4),
since this represents a five-element list.

123

What is the value of

```
(run* q
  (lengtho '(1 0 1) 3))
```

(),
since (1 1) is not 3.

124

What is the value of

```
(run 3 q
  (lengtho q q))
```

(() (1) (0 1)),
since these numbers are the same as their lengths.

What is the value of

(**run** 4 q
  ($length^o$ q q))

125 This expression has no value, since it is still looking for the fourth value.

We could represent both negative and positive integers as `(,*sign-bit* . ,n), where n is our representation of natural numbers. If *sign-bit* is 1, then we have the negative integers and if *sign-bit* is 0, then we have the positive integers. We would still use () to represent zero. And, of course, *sign-bit* could be fresh.

Define sum^o, which expects three integers instead of three natural numbers like $+^o$.

126 That does sound challenging! Perhaps over lunch.

⟹ Now go make yourself a baba ghanoush pita wrap. ⟸

This space reserved for

BABA GHANOUSH STAINS!

8.
Just a Bit More

What is the value of

```
(run 10 (x y r)
  (*o x y r))
```

1
```
((() _0 ())
 ((_0 . _1) () ())
 ((1) (_0 . _1) (_0 . _1))
 ((_0 _1 . _2) (1) (_0 _1 . _2))
 ((0 1) (_0 _1 . _2) (0 _0 _1 . _2))
 ((0 0 1) (_0 _1 . _2) (0 0 _0 _1 . _2))
 ((1 _0 . _1) (0 1) (0 1 _0 . _1))
 ((0 0 0 1) (_0 _1 . _2) (0 0 0 _0 _1 . _2))
 ((1 _0 . _1) (0 0 1) (0 0 1 _0 . _1))
 ((0 1 _0 . _1) (0 1) (0 0 1 _0 . _1))).
```

It is difficult to see patterns when looking at ten values. Would it be easier to examine only its nonground values?

2 Not at all, since the first ten values are nonground.

The value associated with p in

```
(run* p
  (*o '(0 1) '(0 0 1) p))
```

is (0 0 0 1). To which nonground value does this correspond?

3 The fifth nonground value,

```
((0 1) (_0 _1 . _2) (0 _0 _1 . _2)).
```

Describe the fifth nonground value.

4 The product of two and a number greater than one is twice the number.

Describe the seventh nonground value.

5 The product of two and an odd number greater than one is twice the odd number.

Is the product of (1 _0 . _1) and (0 1) odd or even?

6 It is even, since the first bit of (0 1 _0 . _1) is 0.

Is there a nonground value that shows that the product of three and three is nine?

7 No.

What is the value of

```
(run 1 (x y r)
  (≡ `(,x ,y ,r) '((1 1) (1 1) (1 0 0 1)))
  (*ᵒ x y r))
```

8 (((1 1) (1 1) (1 0 0 1))), which shows that the product of three and three is nine.

Here is $*^o$.

```
(defrel (*ᵒ n m p)
  (condᵉ
    ((≡ '() n) (≡ '() p))
    ((posᵒ n) (≡ '() m) (≡ '() p))
    ((≡ '(1) n) (posᵒ m) (≡ m p))
    ((>1ᵒ n) (≡ '(1) m) (≡ n p))
    ((fresh (x z)
       (≡ `(0 . ,x) n) (posᵒ x)
       (≡ `(0 . ,z) p) (posᵒ z)
       (>1ᵒ m)
       (*ᵒ x m z)))
    ((fresh (x y)
       (≡ `(1 . ,x) n) (posᵒ x)
       (≡ `(0 . ,y) m) (posᵒ y)
       (*ᵒ m n p)))
    ((fresh (x y)
       (≡ `(1 . ,x) n) (posᵒ x)
       (≡ `(1 . ,y) m) (posᵒ y)
       (odd-*ᵒ x n m p)))))
```

Describe the first and second **cond**^{e} lines.

9 The first **cond**^{e} line says that the product of zero and anything is zero. The second line says that the product of a positive number and zero is also equal to zero.

Why isn't ((≡ '() *m*) (≡ '() *p*)) the second **cond**^{e} line?

10 If so, the second **cond**^{e} line would also contribute ($n = 0$, $m = 0$, $p = 0$), already contributed by the first line. We would like to avoid duplications. In other words, we enforce the non-overlapping property.

Describe the third and fourth **cond**^{e} lines.	11	The third **cond**^{e} line says that the product of one and a positive number is that number. The fourth **cond**^{e} line says that the product of a number greater than one and one is the number.
Describe the fifth **cond**^{e} line.	12	The fifth **cond**^{e} line says that the product of an even positive number and a number greater than one is an even positive number, using the equation $n \cdot m = 2 \cdot (\frac{n}{2} \cdot m)$.
Why do we use this equation?	13	For the recursion to have a value, one of the arguments to $*^o$ must shrink. Dividing n by two shrinks n.
How do we divide n by two?	14	With ($\equiv$ \`(0 . ,x) n), where x is not ().
Describe the sixth **cond**^{e} line.	15	The sixth **cond**^{e} line says that the product of an odd positive number and an even positive number is the same as the product of the even positive number and the odd positive number.
Describe the seventh **cond**^{e} line.	16	The seventh **cond**^{e} line says that the product of an odd number greater than one and another odd number greater than one is the result of (*odd-*$*^o$ x n m p), where x is $\frac{n-1}{2}$.

Here is *odd-*ᵒ*.

```
(defrel (odd-*o x n m p)
  (fresh (q)
    (bound-*o q p n m)
    (*o x m q)
    (+o `(0 . ,q) m p)))
```

If we ignore *bound-*ᵒ*, what equation describes *odd-*ᵒ*

17 We know that x is $\frac{n-1}{2}$. Therefore, $n \cdot m = 2 \cdot (\frac{n-1}{2} \cdot m) + m$.

Here is a hypothetical definition of *bound-*ᵒ*.

```
(defrel (bound-*o q p n m)
  #s)
```

18 Okay, so this is not the final definition of *bound-*ᵒ*.

Using the hypothetical definition of *bound-*ᵒ*, what values would be associated with n and m in

```
(run 1 (n m)
  (*o n m '(1)))
```

19 ((1) (1)).
This value is contributed by the third **cond**^{e} line of $*^o$.

Now what is the value of

```
(run 1 (n m)
  (>1o n)
  (>1o m)
  (*o n m '(1 1)))
```

20 It has no value,
since ($*^o$ n m '(1 1)) neither succeeds nor fails.

21 Why does ($*^o$ n m '(1 1)) neither succeed nor fail in the previous frame?

Because $*^o$ tries

$$n = 2, 3, 4, \ldots$$

and similarly for m, trying bigger and bigger numbers to see if their product is three. Since there is no bound on how big the numbers can be, $*^o$ tries bigger and bigger numbers forever.

---

22 How can we make ($*^o$ n m '(1 1)) fail in this case?

By redefining *bound-*$*^o$.

---

23 How should *bound-*$*^o$ work?

If we are trying to see if $n * m = r$, then any $n > r$ will not work. So, we can stop searching when n is equal to r. Or, to make it easier to test: ($*^o$ n m r) can only succeed if the lengths (in bits) of n and m do not exceed the length (in bits) of r.

---

24 Here is *bound-*$*^o$.

```
(defrel (bound-*ᵒ q p n m)
  (condᵉ
    ((≡ '() q) (posᵒ p))
    ((fresh (a₀ a₁ a₂ a₃ x y z)
       (≡ `(,a₀ . ,x) q)
       (≡ `(,a₁ . ,y) p)
       (condᵉ
         ((≡ '() n)
          (≡ `(,a₂ . ,z) m)
          (bound-*ᵒ x y z '()))
         ((≡ `(,a₃ . ,z) n)
          (bound-*ᵒ x y z m)))))))
```

Is this definition recursive?

Yes, indeed.

What is the value of

```
(run 2 (n m)
  (*ᵒ n m '(1)))
```

25 (((1) (1))),
because *bound-*ᵒ* fails when the product of n and m is larger than p, and since the length of n plus the length of m is an upper bound on the length of p.

What value is associated with p in

```
(run* p
  (*ᵒ '(1 1 1) '(1 1 1 1 1 1) p))
```

26 (1 0 0 1 1 1 0 1 1),
which contains nine bits.

If we replace a 1 by a 0 in

```
(*ᵒ '(1 1 1) '(1 1 1 1 1 1) p),
```

is nine still the maximum length of p

27 Yes,
because '(1 1 1) and '(1 1 1 1 1 1) represent the largest numbers of lengths three and six, respectively. Of course the rightmost 1 in each number cannot be replaced by a 0.

Here is $=l^o$.

```
(defrel (=lᵒ n m)
  (condᵉ
    ((≡ '() n) (≡ '() m))
    ((≡ '(1) n) (≡ '(1) m))
    ((fresh (a x b y)
       (≡ `(,a . ,x) n) (posᵒ x)
       (≡ `(,b . ,y) m) (posᵒ y)
       (=lᵒ x y)))))
```

Is this definition recursive?

28 Yes, it is.

What is the value of

```
(run* (w x y)
  (=lᵒ `(1 ,w ,x . ,y) '(0 1 1 0 1)))
```

29 $((\_{0}\ \_{1}\ (\_{2}\ 1)))$.
y is $(\_{2}\ 1)$, so the *length* of `(1 ,w ,x . ,y) is the same as the length of (0 1 1 0 1).

What value is associated with b in

(**run*** b
  (=l^o '(1) `(,b)))

30 1,
because if 0 were associated with b, then `(,b) would have become (0), which does not represent a number.

What value is associated with n in

(**run*** n
  (=l^o `(1 0 1 . ,n) '(0 1 1 0 1)))

31 ($\_{0}$ 1),
because if n were ($\_{0}$ 1), then the length of `(1 0 1 . ,n) would be the same as the length of (0 1 1 0 1).

What is the value of

(**run** 5 (y z)
  (=l^o `(1 . ,$y$) `(1 . ,z)))

32 ((() ())
((1) (1))
(($\_{0}$ 1) ($\_{1}$ 1))
(($\_{0}$ $\_{1}$ 1) ($\_{2}$ $\_{3}$ 1))
(($\_{0}$ $\_{1}$ $\_{2}$ 1) ($\_{3}$ $\_{4}$ $\_{5}$ 1))),
because each y and z must be the same length in order for `(1 . ,$y$) and `(1 . ,z) to be the same length.

What is the value of

(**run** 5 (y z)
  (=l^o `(1 . ,$y$) `(0 . ,z)))

33 (((1) (1))
(($\_{0}$ 1) ($\_{1}$ 1))
(($\_{0}$ $\_{1}$ 1) ($\_{2}$ $\_{3}$ 1))
(($\_{0}$ $\_{1}$ $\_{2}$ 1) ($\_{3}$ $\_{4}$ $\_{5}$ 1))
(($\_{0}$ $\_{1}$ $\_{2}$ $\_{3}$ 1) ($\_{4}$ $\_{5}$ $\_{6}$ $\_{7}$ 1))).

Why isn't (() ()) the first value?

34 Because if z were (), then `(0 . ,z) would not represent a number.

What is the value of

```
(run 5 (y z)
  (=lº `(1 • ,y) `(0 1 1 0 1 • ,z)))
```

35
```
(((_0 _1 _2 1) ())
 ((_0 _1 _2 _3 1) (1))
 ((_0 _1 _2 _3 _4 1) (_5 1))
 ((_0 _1 _2 _3 _4 _5 1) (_6 _7 1))
 ((_0 _1 _2 _3 _4 _5 _6 1) (_7 _8 _9 1))).
```

The shortest z is (), which forces y to be a list of length four. Thereafter, as y grows in length, so does z.

Here is $<l^o$.

```
(defrel (<lº n m)
  (condᵉ
    ((≡ '() n) (posº m))
    ((≡ '(1) n) (>1º m))
    ((fresh (a x b y)
       (≡ `(,a • ,x) n) (posº x)
       (≡ `(,b • ,y) m) (posº y)
       (<lº x y)))))
```

How does this definition differ from the definition of $=l^o$

36 In the first **cond**^{e} line, (≡ '() m) is replaced by (pos^o m). In the second **cond**^{e} line, (≡ '(1) m) is replaced by (**>1**^{o} m). This $<l^o$ relation guarantees that n is shorter than m.

What is the value of

```
(run 8 (y z)
  (<lº `(1 • ,y) `(0 1 1 0 1 • ,z)))
```

37
```
((() _0)
 ((1) _0)
 ((_0 1) _1)
 ((_0 _1 1) _2)
 ((_0 _1 _2 1) (_3 • _4))
 ((_0 _1 _2 _3 1) (_4 _5 • _6))
 ((_0 _1 _2 _3 _4 1) (_5 _6 _7 • _8))
 ((_0 _1 _2 _3 _4 _5 1) (_6 _7 _8 _9 • _10))).
```

Why is z fresh in the first four values?

38 A list that represents a number is associated with the variable y. If the length of this list is at most three, then `(1 • ,$y$) is shorter than `(0 1 1 0 1 • ,z), regardless of the value associated with z.

What is the value of

```
(run 1 n
  (<l^o n n))
```

39 It has no value.
The first two $cond^e$ lines fail. In the recursion, x and y are fused with the same fresh variable, which is where we started.

Define $\leqslant l^o$ using $=l^o$ and $<l^o$.

40 Is this correct?

```
(defrel (≤l^o n m)
  (cond^e
    ((=l^o n m))
    ((<l^o n m))))
```

It looks like it might be correct. What is the value of

```
(run 8 (n m)
  (≤l^o n m))
```

41

```
((() ())
 ((1) (1))
 (() (_0 • _1))
 ((_0 1) (_1 1))
 ((1) (_0 _1 • _2))
 ((_0 _1 1) (_2 _3 1))
 ((_0 1) (_1 _2 _3 • _4))
 ((_0 _1 _2 1) (_3 _4 _5 1))).
```

What values are associated with n and m in

```
(run 1 (n m)
  (≤l^o n m)
  (*^o n '(0 1) m))
```

42 (() ()).

What is the value of

```
(run 10 (n m)
  (≤l^o n m)
  (*^o n '(0 1) m))
```

43

```
((() ())
 ((1) (0 1))
 ((0 1) (0 0 1))
 ((1 1) (0 1 1))
 ((1 _0 1) (0 1 _0 1))
 ((0 0 1) (0 0 0 1))
 ((0 1 1) (0 0 1 1))
 ((1 _0 _1 1) (0 1 _0 _1 1))
 ((0 1 _0 1) (0 0 1 _0 1))
 ((0 0 0 1) (0 0 0 0 1))).
```

Now what is the value of

```
(run 9 (n m)
  (≤l^o n m))
```

44

```
((() ())
 ((1) (1))
 (() (_0 . _1))
 ((_0 1) (_1 1))
 ((1) (_0 _1 . _2))
 ((_0 _1 1) (_2 _3 1))
 ((_0 1) (_1 _2 _3 . _4))
 ((_0 _1 _2 1) (_3 _4 _5 1))
 ((_0 _1 1) (_2 _3 _4 _5 . _6))).
```

Do these values include all of the values produced in frame 41?

45 Yes.

Here is $<^o$.

```
(defrel (<^o n m)
  (cond^e
    ((<l^o n m))
    ((=l^o n m)
     (fresh (x)
       (pos^o x)
       (+^o n x m)))))
```

Define $\leqslant^o$ using $<^o$.

46 Here is $\leqslant^o$.

```
(defrel (≤^o n m)
  (cond^e
    ((≡ n m))
    ((<^o n m))))
```

What value is associated with q in

(**run*** q
  ($<^o$ '(1 0 1) '(1 1 1)))

47 $\_{0}$,
since five is less than seven.

What is the value of

(**run*** q
  ($<^o$ '(1 1 1) '(1 0 1)))

48 (),
since seven is not less than five.

What is the value of

(**run*** q
  ($<^o$ '(1 0 1) '(1 0 1)))

49 (),
since five is not less than five. But if we were to replace $<^o$ with $\leqslant^o$, the value would be ($\_{0}$).

What is the value of

(**run** 6 n
  ($<^o$ n '(1 0 1)))

50 (() (1) ($\_{0}$ 1) (0 0 1)),
since ($\_{0}$ 1) represents the numbers two and three.

What is the value of

(**run** 6 m
  ($<^o$ '(1 0 1) m))

51 (($\_{0}$ $\_{1}$ $\_{2}$ $\_{3}$. $\_{4}$) (0 1 1) (1 1 1)),
since ($\_{0}$ $\_{1}$ $\_{2}$ $\_{3}$. $\_{4}$) represents all the numbers greater than seven.

What is the value of

(**run*** n
  ($<^o$ n n))

52 It has no value,
since $<^o$ uses $<l^o$ and we know from frame 39 that ($<l^o$ n n) has no value.

What is the value of

(**run** 4 (n m q r)
  ($\div^o$ n m q r))

53 ((() ($\_{0}$. $\_{1}$) () ())
((1) ($\_{0}$ $\_{1}$. $\_{2}$) () (1))
(($\_{0}$ 1) ($\_{1}$ $\_{2}$ $\_{3}$. $\_{4}$) () ($\_{0}$ 1))
(($\_{0}$ $\_{1}$ 1) ($\_{2}$ $\_{3}$ $\_{4}$ $\_{5}$. $\_{6}$) () ($\_{0}$ $\_{1}$ 1))).
$\div^o$ divides n by m, producing a quotient q and a remainder r.

Define $\div^o$.

54

```
(defrel (÷ᵒ n m q r)
  (condᵉ
    ((≡ '() q) (≡ n r) (<ᵒ n m))
    ((≡ '(1) q) (≡ '() r) (≡ n m)
     (<ᵒ r m))
    ((<ᵒ m n) (<ᵒ r m)
     (fresh (mq)
       (≤lᵒ mq n)
       (*ᵒ m q mq)
       (+ᵒ mq r n))))).
```

With which three cases do the three **cond**^{e} lines correspond?

55 The cases in which the dividend n is less than, equal to, or greater than the divisor m, respectively.

Describe the first **cond**^{e} line.

56 The first **cond**^{e} line divides a number n by a number m greater than n. Therefore the quotient is zero, and the remainder is equal to n.

According to the standard definition of division, division by zero is undefined and the remainder r must always be less than the divisor m. Does the first **cond**^{e} line enforce both of these restrictions?

57 Yes.

The divisor m is greater than the dividend n, which means that m cannot be zero. Also, since m is greater than n and n is equal to r, we know that m is greater than the remainder r. By enforcing the second restriction, we automatically enforce the first.

In the second **cond**^{e} line the dividend and divisor are equal, so the quotient must be one. Why, then, is the $(<^o\ r\ m)$ goal necessary?

58 Because this goal enforces both of the restrictions given in the previous frame.

Describe the first two goals in the third **cond**^{e} line.

59 The goal ($<^o$ m n) ensures that the divisor is less than the dividend, while the goal ($<^o$ r m) enforces the restrictions in frame 57.

Describe the last three goals in the third **cond**^{e} line.

60 The last three goals perform division in terms of multiplication and addition. The equation

$$\frac{n}{m} = q \text{ with remainder } r$$

can be rewritten as

$$n = m \cdot q + r.$$

That is, if mq is the product of m and q, then n is the sum of mq and r. Also, since r cannot be less than zero, mq cannot be greater than n.

Why does the third goal in the last **cond**^{e} line use $\leqslant l^o$ instead of $<^o$

61 Because $\leqslant l^o$ is a closer approximation of $<^o$. If mq is less than or equal to n, then certainly the length of the list representing mq cannot exceed the length of the list representing n.

What is the value of

(run* *m*
  (**fresh** (*r*)
    ($\div^o$ '(1 0 1) *m* '(1 1 1) *r*)))

62 ().

We are trying to find a number m such that dividing five by m produces seven. Of course, we will not be able to find that number.

How is () the value of

(run* *m*
  (**fresh** (*r*)
    ($\div^o$ '(1 0 1) *m* '(1 1 1) *r*)))

63 The third **cond**^{e} line of $\div^o$ ensures that m is less than n when q is greater than one. Thus, $\div^o$ can stop looking for possible values of m when m reaches four.

Why do we need the first two **cond**^{e} lines, given that the third **cond**^{e} line seems so general? Why don't we just remove the first two **cond**^{e} lines and remove the ($<^o$ m n) goal from the third **cond**^{e} line, giving us a simpler definition of $\div^o$

```
(defrel (÷ᵒ n m q r)
  (fresh (mq)
    (<ᵒ r m)
    (≤lᵒ mq n)
    (*ᵒ m q mq)
    (+ᵒ mq r n)))
```

64 Unfortunately, our "improved" definition of $\div^o$ has a problem—the expression

```
(run* m
  (fresh (r)
    (÷ᵒ '(1 0 1) m '(1 1 1) r)))
```

no longer has a value.

Why doesn't the expression

```
(run* m
  (fresh (r)
    (÷ᵒ '(1 0 1) m '(1 1 1) r)))
```

have a value when we use this new definition of $\div^o$

65 Because the new $\div^o$ does not ensure that m is less than n when q is greater than one. Thus, this new $\div^o$ never stops trying to find an m such that dividing five by m produces seven.

⇒ Hold on! It's going to get subtle! ⇐

What is the value of this expression when using the original definition of $\div^o$, as defined in frame 54?

```
(run 3 (y z)
  (÷ᵒ `(1 0 . ,y) '(0 1) z '()))
```

66 It has no value.
We cannot divide an odd number by two and get a remainder of zero. The original definition of $\div^o$ never stops looking for values of y and z that satisfy the division relation, although there are no such values. Instead, we would like it to fail immediately.

How can we define a better version of $\div^o$, one that allows the **run*** expression in frame 66 to have a value?

67 Since a number is represented as a list of bits, let's break up the problem by splitting the list into two parts—the "head" and the "rest."

Good idea! How exactly can we split up a number?

68 If n is a positive number, we split it into parts *nhigh*, which might be 0 and *nlow*. $n = nhigh \cdot 2^p + nlow$, where *nlow* has at most p bits.

That's right! We can perform this task using $split^o$.

```
(defrel (splito n r l h)
  (conde
    ((≡ '() n) (≡ '() h) (≡ '() l))
    ((fresh (b n̂)
       (≡ `(0 ,b . ,n̂) n) (≡ '() r)
       (≡ `(,b . ,n̂) h) (≡ '() l)))
    ((fresh (n̂)
       (≡ `(1 . ,n̂) n) (≡ '() r)
       (≡ n̂ h) (≡ '(1) l)))
    ((fresh (b n̂ a r̂)
       (≡ `(0 ,b . ,n̂) n)
       (≡ `(,a . ,r̂) r) (≡ '() l)
       (splito `(,b . ,n̂) r̂ '() h)))
    ((fresh (n̂ a r̂)
       (≡ `(1 . ,n̂) n)
       (≡ `(,a . ,r̂) r) (≡ '(1) l)
       (splito n̂ r̂ '() h)))
    ((fresh (b n̂ a r̂ l̂)
       (≡ `(,b . ,n̂) n)
       (≡ `(,a . ,r̂) r)
       (≡ `(,b . ,l̂) l)
       (poso l̂)
       (splito n̂ r̂ l̂ h)))))
```

What does $split^o$ do?

69 ($split^o$ n '() l h) *moves* the lowest bit† of n, if any, into l, and moves the remaining bits of n into h; ($split^o$ n '(1) l h) moves the two lowest bits of n into l and moves the remaining bits of n into h; and ($split^o$ n '(1 1 1 1) l h), ($split^o$ n '(0 1 1 1) l h), or ($split^o$ n '(0 0 0 1) l h) move the five lowest bits of n into l and move the remaining bits into h; and so on.

† The lowest bit of a positive number n is the *car* of n.

What else does *split*^{o} do?

70 Since *split*^{o} is a relation, it can construct *n* by combining the lower-order bits of *l* with the higher-order bits of *h*, inserting *padding* (using the length of *r*) bits.

Why is *split*^{o}'s definition so complicated?

71 Because *split*^{o} must not allow the list (0) to represent a number. For example, (*split*^{o} '(0 0 1) '() '() '(0 1)) should succeed, but (*split*^{o} '(0 0 1) '() '(0) '(0 1)) should not.

How does *split*^{o} ensure that (0) is not constructed?

72 By removing the rightmost zeros after splitting the number *n* into its lower-order bits and its higher-order bits.

What is the value of

```
(run* (l h)
  (splito '(0 0 1 0 1) '() l h))
```

73 ((() (0 1 0 1))).

What is the value of

```
(run* (l h)
  (splito '(0 0 1 0 1) '(1) l h))
```

74 ((() (1 0 1))).

What is the value of

```
(run* (l h)
  (splito '(0 0 1 0 1) '(0 1) l h))
```

75 (((0 0 1) (0 1))).

What is the value of

```
(run* (l h)
  (splito '(0 0 1 0 1) '(1 1) l h))
```

76 (((0 0 1) (0 1))).

What is the value of

```
(run* (r l h)
  (splito '(0 0 1 0 1) r l h))
```

77

```
((() () (0 1 0 1))
 ((_0) () (1 0 1))
 ((_0 _1) (0 0 1) (0 1))
 ((_0 _1 _2) (0 0 1) (1))
 ((_0 _1 _2 _3) (0 0 1 0 1) ())
 ((_0 _1 _2 _3 _4 • _5) (0 0 1 0 1) ())).
```

Now we are ready for division! If we split n (the divisor) in two parts, *nhigh* and *nlow*, it stands to reason that q is also split into *qhigh* and *qlow*.

78 Then what?

Remember, $n = m \cdot q + r$. Substituting $n = nhigh \cdot 2^p + nlow$ and $q = qhigh \cdot 2^p + qlow$ yields $nhigh \cdot 2^p + nlow = m \cdot qhigh \cdot 2^p + m \cdot qlow + r$.

79 Okay.

Then what should happen?

We try to divide *nhigh* by m obtaining *qhigh* and *rhigh*: $nhigh = m \cdot qhigh + rhigh$ from which we get $nhigh \cdot 2^p = m \cdot qhigh \cdot 2^p + rhigh \cdot 2^p$. Subtracting from the original, we obtain the relation $nlow = m \cdot qlow + r - rhigh \cdot 2^p$, which means that $m \cdot qlow + r - nlow$ must be divisible by 2^p and the result is *rhigh*. The advantage is that when checking the latter two equations, the numbers *nlow*, *qlow*, and so on, are all range-limited, and must fit within p bits. We can therefore check the equations without danger of trying higher and higher numbers forever. Now we can just define our arithmetic relations by directly using these equations.

80 Okay.

Here is an improved definition of $\div^o$ which is more sophisticated than the ones given in frames 54 and 64. All three definitions implement division with remainder, which means that ($\div^o$ *n m q r*) satisfies $n = m \cdot q + r$ with $0 \leqslant r < m$.

```
(defrel (÷ᵒ n m q r)
  (condᵉ
    ((≡ '() q) (≡ r n) (<ᵒ n m))
    ((≡ '(1) q) (=lᵒ m n) (+ᵒ r m n)
     (<ᵒ r m))
    ((posᵒ q) (<lᵒ m n) (<ᵒ r m)
     (n-wider-than-mᵒ n m q r))))
```

Does the redefined $\div^o$ use any new helper relations?

81 Yes,
the new $\div^o$ relies on *n-wider-than-m*^{o}, which itself relies on *split*^{o}.

```
(defrel (n-wider-than-mᵒ n m q r)
  (fresh (n_high n_low q_high q_low)
    (fresh (mq_low mrq_low rr r_high)
      (splitᵒ n r n_low n_high)
      (splitᵒ q r q_low q_high)
      (condᵉ
        ((≡ '() n_high)
         (≡ '() q_high)
         (−ᵒ n_low r mq_low)
         (*ᵒ m q_low mq_low))
        ((posᵒ n_high)
         (*ᵒ m q_low mq_low)
         (+ᵒ r mq_low mrq_low)
         (−ᵒ mrq_low n_low rr)
         (splitᵒ rr r '() r_high)
         (÷ᵒ n_high m q_high r_high))))))
```

What is the value of this expression when using the original definition of $\div^o$, as defined in frame 54?

```
(run 3 (y z)
  (÷ᵒ `(1 0 . ,y) '(0 1) z '()))
```

82 It has no value.
We cannot divide an odd number by two and get a remainder of zero. The original definition of $\div^o$ never stops looking for values of *y* and *z* that satisfy the division relation, even though there are no such values. Instead, we would like it to fail immediately.

Describe the latest version of $\div^o$.

83 This version of $\div^o$ fails when it determines that the relation cannot hold. For example, dividing the number $6 + 8 \cdot k$ by 4 does not have a remainder of 0 or 1, for all possible values of k.

Here is log^o with its three helper relations.

```
(defrel (logᵒ n b q r)
  (condᵉ
    ((≡ '() q) (≤ᵒ n b)
     (+ᵒ r '(1) n))
    ((≡ '(1) q) (>1ᵒ b) (=lᵒ n b)
     (+ᵒ r b n))
    ((≡ '(1) b) (posᵒ q)
     (+ᵒ r '(1) n))
    ((≡ '() b) (posᵒ q) (≡ r n))
    ((≡ '(0 1) b)
     (fresh (a ad dd)
       (posᵒ dd)
       (≡ `(,a ,ad . ,dd) n)
       (exp2ᵒ n '() q)
       (fresh (s)
         (splitᵒ n dd r s))))
    ((≤ᵒ '(1 1) b) (<lᵒ b n)
     (base-three-or-moreᵒ n b q r))))

(defrel (exp2ᵒ n b q)
  (condᵉ
    ((≡ '(1) n) (≡ '() q))
    ((>1ᵒ n) (≡ '(1) q)
     (fresh (s)
       (splitᵒ n b s '(1))))
    ((fresh (q₁ b₂)
       (≡ `(0 . ,q₁) q) (posᵒ q₁)
       (<lᵒ b n)
       (appendᵒ b `(1 . ,b) b₂)
       (exp2ᵒ n b₂ q₁)))
    ((fresh (q₁ n_high b₂ s)
       (≡ `(1 . ,q₁) q) (posᵒ q₁)
       (posᵒ n_high)
       (splitᵒ n b s n_high)
       (appendᵒ b `(1 . ,b) b₂)
       (exp2ᵒ n_high b₂ q₁)))))
```

84 The relations $base\text{-}three\text{-}or\text{-}more^o$ and $repeated\text{-}mul^o$ require some thinking.

```
(defrel (base-three-or-moreᵒ n b q r)
  (fresh (bw₁ bw nw nw₁ q_low1 q_low s)
    (exp2ᵒ b '() bw₁)
    (+ᵒ bw₁ '(1) bw)
    (<lᵒ q n)
    (fresh (q₁ bwq₁)
      (+ᵒ q '(1) q₁)
      (*ᵒ bw q₁ bwq₁)
      (<ᵒ nw₁ bwq₁))
    (exp2ᵒ n '() nw₁)
    (+ᵒ nw₁ '(1) nw)
    (÷ᵒ nw bw q_low1 s)
    (+ᵒ q_low '(1) q_low1)
    (≤lᵒ q_low q)
    (fresh (bq_low q_high s qd_high qd)
      (repeated-mulᵒ b q_low bq_low)
      (÷ᵒ nw bw₁ q_high s)
      (+ᵒ q_low qd_high q_high)
      (+ᵒ q_low qd q)
      (≤ᵒ qd qd_high)
      (fresh (bqd bq₁ bq)
        (repeated-mulᵒ b qd bqd)
        (*ᵒ bq_low bqd bq)
        (*ᵒ b bq bq₁)
        (+ᵒ bq r n)
        (<ᵒ n bq₁)))))

(defrel (repeated-mulᵒ n q nq)
  (condᵉ
    ((posᵒ n) (≡ '() q) (≡ '(1) nq))
    ((≡ '(1) q) (≡ n nq))
    ((>1ᵒ q)
     (fresh (q₁ nq₁)
       (+ᵒ q₁ '(1) q)
       (repeated-mulᵒ n q₁ nq₁)
       (*ᵒ nq₁ n nq)))))
```

Guess what log^o does?

85 It builds a split-rail fence.

Not quite. Try again.

86 It implements the logarithm relation: (log^o n b q r) holds if $n = b^q + r$.

Are there any other conditions that the logarithm relation must satisfy?

87 There had better be!

Otherwise, the relation would always hold if $q = 0$ and $r = n - 1$, regardless of the value of b.

Give the complete logarithm relation.

88 (log^o n b q r) holds if $n = b^q + r$, where $0 \leqslant r$ and q is the largest number that satisfies the relation.

Does the logarithm relation look familiar?

89 Yes.

The logarithm relation is similar to the division relation, but with exponentiation in place of multiplication.

In which ways are log^o and $\div^o$ similar?

90 Both log^o and $\div^o$ are relations that take four arguments, each of which could be fresh. The $\div^o$ relation can be used to define the $*^o$ relation—the remainder must be zero, and the zero divisor case must be accounted for. Also, $\div^o$ can be used to define the $+^o$ relation.

The log^o relation is equally flexible, and can be used to define exponentiation, to determine exact discrete logarithms, and even to determine discrete logarithms with a *remainder*. The log^o relation can also find the base b that corresponds to a given n and q.

91

What value is associated with *r* in

```
(run* r
  (logᵒ '(0 1 1 1) '(0 1) '(1 1) r))
```

(0 1 1),
since $14 = 2^3 + 6$.

92

What is the value of

```
(run 9 (b q r)
  (logᵒ '(0 0 1 0 0 0 1) b q r)
  (>1ᵒ q))
```

```
((() (_0 _1 . _2) (0 0 1 0 0 0 1))
 ((1) (_0 _1 . _2) (1 1 0 0 0 0 1))
 ((0 1) (0 1 1) (0 0 1))
 ((1 1) (1 1) (1 0 0 1 0 1))
 ((0 0 1) (1 1) (0 0 1))
 ((0 0 0 1) (0 1) (0 0 1))
 ((1 0 1) (0 1) (1 1 0 1 0 1))
 ((0 1 1) (0 1) (0 0 0 0 0 1))
 ((1 1 1) (0 1) (1 1 0 0 1))),
```

since
$68 = 0^n + 68$ where $n > 1$,
$68 = 1^n + 67$ where $n > 1$,
$68 = 2^6 + 4$,
$68 = 3^3 + 41$,
$68 = 4^3 + 4$,
$68 = 8^2 + 4$,
$68 = 5^2 + 43$,
$68 = 6^2 + 32$, and
$68 = 7^2 + 19$.

93

Define *exp*ᵒ using *log*ᵒ.

```
(defrel (expᵒ b q n)
  (logᵒ n b q '()))
```

94

What value is associated with *t* in

```
(run* t
  (expᵒ '(1 1) '(1 0 1) t))
```

(1 1 0 0 1 1 1 1),
which is the same as (*build-num* 243).

⟹ Addition can be defined using $\div^o$ (frame 90). ⟸

⟹ Define addition using only cond^e, $\equiv$, $<^o$, and $\div^o$. ⟸

9.
Thin Ice

1 Does

(**cond**^{a}
(#u #s)
(#s #u))

succeed?†

No,
because the first goal of the first **cond**^{a} line is the goal #u, so **cond**^{a} tries the second line. In the spirit of **cond**, we refer to the first goal of a **cond**^{a} line as its *question*, and the rest of the goals as its *answer*.

† **cond**^{a} is written conda and is pronounced "con-day." **cond**^{a} is like the so-called *soft-cut* (also known as *if-then-else*) and is described on page 45 of William F. Clocksin. *Clause and Effect.* Springer, 1997.

---

2 Does

(**cond**^{a}
(#u #s)
(#s #s))

succeed?

Yes,
because the question of the first **cond**^{a} line is the goal #u, so **cond**^{a} tries the second line.

---

3 Does

(**cond**^{a}
(#s #u)
(#s #s))

succeed?

No,
because the question of the first **cond**^{a} line is the goal #s, so **cond**^{a} tries the answer of the first line.

---

4 Does

(**cond**^{a}
(#s #s)
(#s #u))

succeed?

Yes,
because the question of the first **cond**^{a} line is the goal #s, so **cond**^{a} tries the answer of the first line.

What is the value of

```
(run* x
  (conda
    ((≡ 'olive x) #s)
    (#s (≡ 'oil x))))
```

5 (olive),
because (≡ 'olive x) succeeds; therefore, **cond**^{a} tries the answer of the first **cond**^{a} line, which is #s. The #s preserves the association of olive to x.
What does the "*a*" in **cond**^{a} stand for?

The Law of cond^a

The first cond^a line whose question succeeds is the only line that can contribute values.

It stands for *a* single line, since at most a single line can succeed.

6 Hmm, interesting.

What is the value of

```
(run* x
  (conda
    ((≡ 'virgin x) #u)
    ((≡ 'olive x) #s)
    (#s (≡ 'oil x))))
```

7 (),
because (≡ 'virgin x) succeeds, we get to assume that the remaining two **cond**^{a} lines no longer can contribute values. So, when the **cond**^{a} line fails, the entire **cond**^{a} expression fails.

This is a big difference from *every* **cond**^{e} line contributing values to *exactly one* **cond**^{a} line possibly contributing values when the first successful question is discovered.

What is the value of

```
(run* q
  (fresh (x y)
    (≡ 'split x)
    (≡ 'pea y)
    (conda
      ((≡ 'split x) (≡ x y))
      (#s #s))))
```

8 ().

The (≡ 'split x) question in the **cond**^{a} expression succeeds, since split is already associated with x. The answer, (≡ x y), fails, however, because x and y are associated with different values.

What is the value of

```
(run* q
  (fresh (x y)
    (≡ 'split x)
    (≡ 'pea y)
    (conda
      ((≡ x y) (≡ 'split x))
      (#s #s))))
```

9 ($\_{0}$).

(≡ x y) fails, since x and y are associated with different values. The question of the first **cond**^{a} line fails, therefore we try the second **cond**^{a} line, which succeeds.

Why does the value change when we switch the order of (≡ 'split x) and (≡ x y) within the first **cond**^{a} line?

10 Because only if the question of a **cond**^{a} line fails do we consider the remaining **cond**^{a} lines. If the question succeeds, it is as if the remaining **cond**^{a} lines have been replaced by a single (#s #u).

Consider the definition of *not-pasta*^{o}.

```
(defrel (not-pastao x)
  (conda
    ((≡ 'pasta x) #u)
    (#s #s)))
```

What is the value of

```
(run* x
  (conda
    ((not-pastao x) #u)
    ((≡ 'spaghetti x) #s)))
```

11 (spaghetti),

because x starts out fresh, but the question (*not-pasta*^{o} x) associates x with 'pasta, but then fails. Since (*not-pasta*^{o} x) fails, we try (≡ 'spaghetti x).

Then, what is the value of

```
(run* x
  (≡ 'spaghetti x)
  (conda
    ((not-pastao x) #u)
    ((≡ 'spaghetti x) #s)))
```

12 (),
because (*not-pasta*^{o} x) succeeds, which shows the risks involved when using **cond**^{a}. We can't allow a fresh variable to become associated as part of a **cond**^{a} question.

The Second Commandment (Initial)

If prior to determining the question of a cond^a line a variable is fresh, it must remain fresh in that line's question.

What is the value of

```
(run* q
  (conda
    ((alwayso) #s)
    (#s #u)))
```

13 It has no value,
since **run*** never finishes building the list of $_{-0}$s.

What is the value of†

```
(run* q
  (condu
    ((alwayso) #s)
    (#s #u)))
```

14 ($_{-0}$),
because **cond**^{u} is like **cond**^{a}, except that the successful question, here (*always*^{o}), succeeds exactly once.

† **cond**^{u} is written condu and is pronounced "cond-you." **cond**^{u} corresponds to Mercury's committed choice (so-called *once*), which is described in Fergus Henderson, Thomas Conway, Zoltan Somogyi, and David Jeffery. "The Mercury language reference manual." University of Melbourne Technical Report 96/10, 1996. Mercury was the first language to effectively combine and extensively use soft-cuts as in frame 1 and committed choice, avoiding the *cut* of Prolog. See Lee Naish. "Pruning in logic programming." University of Melbourne Technical Report 95/16, 1995.

What is the value of

```
(run* q
  (condu
    (#s (alwayso))
    (#s #u)))
```

15 It has no value,
since **run*** never finishes building the list of $_{0}$s.
What does the "*u*" in **cond**^{u} stand for?

It stands for *uni-*, because the successful *question* of a **cond**^{u} line succeeds exactly once.

16 Hmm, interesting.

What is the value of

```
(run 1 q
  (conda
    ((alwayso) #s)
    (#s #u))
  #u)
```

17 It has no value, since the outer #u fails each time (*always*^{o}) succeeds.

What is the value of

```
(run 1 q
  (condu
    ((alwayso) #s)
    (#s #u))
  #u)
```

18 (),
because **cond**^{u}'s successful question, (*always*^{o}), succeeds only once.

The Law of cond^u

cond^u behaves like cond^a, except that a successful question succeeds only once.

Does **cond**^{u} need a commandment, too?

[19] Yes it does.

The Second Commandment (Final)

If prior to determining the question of a cond^a or cond^u line a variable is fresh, it must remain fresh in that line's question.

Here is *teacup*^{o} once again, using **cond**^{e} rather than $disj_2$ as in frame 1:82.

```
(defrel (teacupᵒ t)
  (condᵉ
    ((≡ 'tea t))
    ((≡ 'cup t))))
```

[20] Sure.

Here is *once*^{o}.

```
(defrel (onceᵒ g)
  (condᵘ
    (g #s)
    (#s #u)))
```

What is the value of

```
(run* x
  (onceᵒ (teacupᵒ x)))
```

[21] (tea).
The first **cond**^{e} line of *teacup*^{o} succeeds. Since *once*^{o}'s goal can succeed only once, there are no more values. But, **The Second Commandment** is broken by this use of *once*^{o}.

What is the value of

```
(run* r
  (condᵉ
    ((teacupᵒ r) #s)
    ((≡ #f r) #s)))
```

[22] (#f tea cup).

What is the value of

```
(run* r
  (conda
    ((teacupo r) #s)
    (#s (≡ #f r))))
```

23 (tea cup).
But the question in the first **cond**[a] line breaks **The Second Commandment**.

And, what is the value of

```
(run* r
  (≡ #f r)
  (conda
    ((teacupo r) #s)
    ((≡ #f r) #s)
    (#s #u)))
```

24 (#f),
since this value is included in frame 22.

What is the value of

```
(run* r
  (≡ #f r)
  (condu
    ((teacupo r) #s)
    ((≡ #f r) #s)
    (#s #u)))
```

25 (#f).
More arithmetic?

Sure. Here is *bump*[o].

```
(defrel (bumpo n x)
  (conde
    ((≡ n x))
    ((fresh (m)
       (-o n '(1) m)
       (bumpo m x)))))
```

What is the value of

```
(run* x
  (bumpo '(1 1 1) x))
```

26
```
((1 1 1)
 (0 1 1)
 (1 0 1)
 (0 0 1)
 (1 1)
 (0 1)
 (1)
 ()).
```

Here is *gen&test*$+^o$.

```
(defrel (gen&test+ᵒ i j k)
  (onceᵒ
    (fresh (x y z)
      (+ᵒ x y z)
      (≡ i x)
      (≡ j y)
      (≡ k z))))
```

What is the value of

```
(run* q
  (gen&test+ᵒ '(0 0 1) '(1 1) '(1 1 1)))
```

27 $(\_{0})$
because four plus three is seven, but there is more.

What values are associated with x, y, and z after $(+^o\ x\ y\ z)$

28 $\_{0}$, (), and $\_{0}$, since x and z have been fused.

What happens next?

29 $(\equiv i\ x)$ succeeds.
(0 0 1) is associated with i and is fused with the fresh x. As a result, (0 0 1) is associated with x.

What happens after $(\equiv i\ x)$ succeeds?

30 $(\equiv j\ y)$ fails,
since (1 1) is associated with j and () is associated with y.

What happens after $(\equiv j\ y)$ fails?

31 $(+^o\ x\ y\ z)$ is tried again, and this time associates () with x, and this pair $(\_{0} \cdot \_{1})$ with both y and z.

What happens next?

32 $(\equiv i\ x)$ fails,
since (0 0 1) is still associated with i and () is associated with x.

What happens after $(\equiv i\ x)$ fails?

33 $(+^{o}\ x\ y\ z)$ is tried again and this time associating (1) with the fused x and y. Finally, (0 1) is associated with z.

What happens next?

34 $(\equiv i\ x)$ fails,
since (0 0 1) is still associated with i and (1) is associated with x.

What happens the 230th time that $(+^{o}\ x\ y\ z)$ is used?

35 $(+^{o}\ x\ y\ z)$ associates (0 0 $\_{0}$ • $\_{1}$), with x, (1 1) with y, and (1 1 $\_{0}$ • $\_{1}$), with z.

What happens next?

36 $(\equiv i\ x)$ succeeds,
associating (0 0 1) with x and therefore (1 1 1) with z.

What happens after $(\equiv i\ x)$ succeeds?

37 $(\equiv j\ y)$ succeeds,
since (1 1) is associated with the fused j and y.

What happens after $(\equiv j\ y)$ succeeds?

38 $(\equiv k\ z)$ succeeds,
since (1 1 1) is associated with the fused k and z.

What values are associated with x, y, and z before $(+^{o}\ x\ y\ z)$ is used in the body of *gen&test*$+^{o}$

39 There are no values associated with x, y, and z since they are fresh.

What is the value of

```
(run 1 q
  (gen&test+o
    '(0 0 1) '(1 1) '(0 1 1)))
```

40 It has no value.

---

41 Can $(+^o\ x\ y\ z)$ fail when x, y, and z are fresh?

Never.

---

42 Why doesn't

```
(run 1 q
  (gen&test+o
    '(0 0 1) '(1 1) '(0 1 1)))
```

have a value?

In *gen&test*$+^o$, $(+^o\ x\ y\ z)$ *generates* various associations for x, y, and z. Next, $(\equiv i\ x)$, $(\equiv j\ y)$, and $(\equiv k\ z)$ *test* if the given triple of values i, j, and k is present among the generated triple x, y, and z. All the generated triples satisfy, by definition, the relation $+^o$. If the triple of values i, j, and k is chosen so that $i + j$ is not equal to k, and our definition of $+^o$ is correct, then that triple of values cannot be found among those generated by $+^o$.

$(+^o\ x\ y\ z)$ continues to generate associations, and the tests $(\equiv i\ x)$, $(\equiv j\ y)$, and $(\equiv k\ z)$ continue to reject them. So this **run 1** expression has no value.

---

43 Here is *enumerate*$+^o$.

```
(defrel (enumerate+o r n)
  (fresh (i j k)
    (bumpo n i)
    (bumpo n j)
    (+o i j k)
    (gen&test+o i j k)
    (≡ `(,i ,j ,k) r)))
```

What is the value of

```
(run* s
  (enumerate+o s '(1 1)))
```

```
((() (1 1) (1 1))
 ((1 1) () (1 1))
 ((1 1) (1 1) (0 1 1))
 (() (0 1) (0 1))
 ((1 1) (0 1) (1 0 1))
 (() (1) (1))
 ((1 1) (1) (0 0 1))
 ((1) (1 1) (0 0 1))
 (() () ())
 ((1) (1) (0 1))
 ((1) (0 1) (1 1))
 ((0 1) () (0 1))
 ((1) () (1))
 ((0 1) (0 1) (0 0 1))
 ((0 1) (1 1) (1 0 1))
 ((0 1) (1) (1 1))).
```

Describe the values in the previous frame.	44	The values can be thought of as four groups of four values. Within the first group, the first value is always (); within the second group, the first value is always (1); etc. Then, within each group, the second value ranges from () to (1 1). And the third value, of course, is the sum of the first two values.
What is true about the value in frame 43?	45	It appears to contain all triples of values of i, j, and k, where $i + j = k$ with i and j ranging from () to (1 1).
All such triples?	46	It seems so.
Can we be certain without counting and analyzing the values? Can we be sure just knowing that there is at least one value?	47	That's confusing.
Okay, suppose one of the triples, ((0 1) (1 1) (1 0 1)), were missing.	48	But how could that be? We know (*bump^o* n i) associates the numbers within the range () through n with i. So if we try it enough times, we eventually get all such numbers. The same is true for (*bump^o* n j). So, we definitely determine ($+^o$ i j k) when (0 1) is associated with i and (1 1) is associated with j, which then associates (1 0 1) with k. We have already seen that.
Then what happens?	49	Then we try to determine if (*gen&test+^{o}* i j k) can succeed, where (0 1) is associated with i, (1 1) is associated with j, and (1 0 1) is associated with k.

At least once?

50 Yes,
since we are interested in only one value. After $(+^o\ x\ y\ z)$, we check that (0 1) is associated with x, (1 1) with y, and (1 0 1) with z. If not, we try $(+^o\ x\ y\ z)$ again, and again.

What if such a triple were found?

51 Then *gen&test*$+^o$ would succeed, producing the triple as the result of *enumerate*$+^o$. Then, because the **fresh** expression in *gen&test*$+^o$ is wrapped in a *once*^{o}, we would pick a new pair of i-j values, etc.

What if we were unable to find such a triple?

52 Then the **run** expression would have no value.

Why would it have no value?

53 If no result of $(+^o\ x\ y\ z)$ matches the desired triple, then, as in frame 40, we would keep trying $(+^o\ x\ y\ z)$ forever.

So can we say, just by glancing at the value in frame 43, that

```
(run* s
  (enumerate+o s '(1 1)))
```

produces all triples i, j, and k such that $i + j = k$, for i and j ranging from () to (1 1)?

54 Yes, that's clear.
If one triple were missing, we would have no value at all!

So what does *enumerate*$+^o$ determine?

55 It determines that $(+^o\ x\ y\ z)$ with x, y, and z being fresh eventually generates *all* triples, where $x + y = z$. At least, *enumerate*$+^o$ determines that for x and y being () through some n.

What is the value of

```
(run 1 s
  (enumerate+ᵒ s '(1 1 1)))
```

56 ((() (1 1 1) (1 1 1))).

Do we need *gen&test+ᵒ*

57 Not at all.
The same variables i, j, and k that are arguments to *gen&test+ᵒ* can be found in the **fresh** expression in *enumerate+ᵒ*, so we can replace (*gen&test+ᵒ* i j k) with the *onceᵒ* expression unchanged in *enumerate+ᵒ*.

Here is the new *enumerate+ᵒ*.

```
(defrel (enumerate+ᵒ r n)
  (fresh (i j k)
    (bumpᵒ n i)
    (bumpᵒ n j)
    (+ᵒ i j k)
    (onceᵒ
      (fresh (x y z)
        (+ᵒ x y z)
        (≡ i x)
        (≡ j y)
        (≡ k z)))
    (≡ `(,i ,j ,k) r)))
```

58 Now that we have this new *enumerate+ᵒ*, can we also use *enumerate+ᵒ* with *ᵒ and *expᵒ*.

59 Yes, if we rename it and include an operator argument, *op*.

Define *enumerate*^{o} so that *op* is an expected argument.

Here is *enumerate*^{o}.

```
(defrel (enumerateᵒ op r n)
  (fresh (i j k)
    (bumpᵒ n i)
    (bumpᵒ n j)
    (op i j k)
    (onceᵒ
      (fresh (x y z)
        (op x y z)
        (≡ i x)
        (≡ j y)
        (≡ k z)))
    (≡ `(,i ,j ,k) r)))
```

But, what about $\div^o$ and *log*^{o}?

60 The *op* argument of *enumerate*^{o} expects three arguments. But, $\div^o$ and *log*^{o} expect *four* arguments. This proposed variant of *enumerate*^{o} would need two additional fresh variables: one for the outer **fresh**, say h, and one for the inner **fresh**, say w.

The rest should follow naturally, right?

Ready to look under the hood?

10.
Under the Hood

1 Now it is time to understand the core of $\equiv$, **fresh**, **cond**^{e}, **run**, **run***, and **defrel**.

What about **cond**^{a} and **cond**^{u}?

2 Of course, we show the core of **cond**^{a} and **cond**^{u} as well.

Shall we begin with $\equiv$?

3 Sure! The definition of $\equiv$ relies on *unify*, which we shall discuss soon. But we'll need a few new ideas first.

Okay, let's begin.

4 Here is how we create a unique† variable.

```
(define (var name) (vector name))
```

Define *var?*

† *vector* creates a vector, a datatype distinct from pairs, strings, characters, numbers, Booleans, symbols, and (). Each use of *var* creates a new one-element vector representing a unique variable. We ignore the vectors' contents, instead distinguishing vectors by their addresses in memory. We could instead distinguish variables by their values, provided we ensure their values are unique (for example, using a unique natural number in each variable).

And here is a simple definition of *var?*.

```
(define (var? x) (vector? x))
```

5 We create three variables *u*, *v*, and *w*.

```
(define u (var 'u))

(define v (var 'v))

(define w (var 'w))
```

Define the variables *x*, *y*, and *z*.

Okay, here are the variables *x*, *y*, and *z*.

```
(define x (var 'x))

(define y (var 'y))

(define z (var 'z))
```

The pair `(,z . a) is an *association* of a with the variable *z*.

6 When is a pair an association?

When the *car* of that pair is a variable. The *cdr* of an association may be itself a variable or a value that contains zero or more variables. What is the value of

(*cdr* `(,z . b))

7 b.

What is the value of

(*cdr* `(,z . (,x e ,y)))

8 The list `(,x e ,y).

The list

`((,z . oat) (,x . nut))

is a *substitution*.

9 What is a substitution?

A substitution† is a special kind of list of associations. In the substitution

`((,x . ,z))

what does the association `(,x . ,z) represent?

† These substitutions are known as *triangular* substitutions. For more on these substitutions see Franz Baader and Wayne Snyder. "Unification theory," Chapter 8 of *Handbook of Automated Reasoning*, edited by John Alan Robinson and Andrei Voronkov. Elsevier Science and MIT Press, 2001.

10 In a substitution, an association whose *cdr* is also a variable represents the fusing of that association's two variables.

Here is *empty-s*.

```
(define empty-s '())
```

What is *empty-s*

11 The substitution that contains no associations.

Is `((,z . a) (,x . ,w) (,z . b)) a substitution?	12 Not here, since our substitutions cannot contain two or more associations with the same *car*.
What is the value of (*walk* *z* `((,z . a) (,x . ,w) (,y . ,z)))	13 a, because we look up *z* in the substitution (*walk*'s second argument) to find its association, `(,z . a), and *walk* produces this association's *cdr*, a, since a is not a variable.
What is the value of (*walk* *y* `((,z . a) (,x . ,w) (,y . ,z)))	14 a, because we look up *y* in the substitution to find its association, `(,y . ,z) and we look up *z* in the same substitution to find its association, `(,z . a), and *walk* produces this association's *cdr*, a, since a is not a variable.
What is the value of (*walk* *x* `((,z . a) (,x . ,w) (,y . ,z)))	15 The variable *w*, because we look up *x* in the substitution to find its association, `(,x . ,w), and produce its association's *cdr*, *w*, because the variable *w* is not the *car* of any association in the substitution.

The value of the expression below is y.

(*walk* x
  `((,x . ,y) (,v . ,x) (,w . ,x)))

What are the walks of v and w

16 Their values are also y.
When we look up the variable v (respectively, w) in the substitution, we find the association `(,$v$ . ,$x$) (respectively, `(,w . ,x)) and we know what happens when we walk x in this substitution.

What is the value of

(*walk* w
  `((,x . b) (,z . ,y) (,w . (,x e ,z))))

17 The list `(,x e ,z).

Here is *walk*, which relies on *assv*. *assv* is a function that expects a value v and a list of associations l. *assv* either produces the first association in l that has v as its *car* using *eqv?*, or produces #f if l has no such association.

```
(define (walk v s)
  (let ((a (and (var? v) (assv v s))))
    (cond
      ((pair? a) (walk (cdr a) s))
      (else v))))
```

When is *walk* recursive?

18 When a is an association rather than #f.

What property holds when a variable has been *walk*'d?

19 If a variable has been *walk*'d in a substitution s, and *walk* has produced a variable x, then we know that x is fresh.

Here are *ext-s* and *occurs?*.

```
(define (ext-s x v s)
  (cond
    ((occurs? x v s)† #f)
    (else (cons `(,x . ,v) s))))

(define (occurs? x v s)
  (let ((v (walk v s)))
    (cond
      ((var? v) (eqv? v x))
      ((pair? v)
       (or (occurs? x (car v) s)
           (occurs? x (cdr v) s)))
      (else #f))))
```

Describe the behavior of *ext-s*.

† This expression tests whether or not x occurs in v, using the substitution s. It is also called the *occurs check*. See frames 1:47–49.

20 *ext-s* either extends a substitution s with an association between the variable x and the value v, or it produces #f if extending the substitution with the pair `(,x . ,v) would have created a *cycle*.

Is

`((,z . a) (,x . ,x) (,y . ,z))

a substitution?

21 Not here,
since we forbid a substitution from containing a cycle like `(,x . ,x) in which its *car* is the same as its *cdr*.

Is

`((,x . ,y) (,w . a) (,z . ,x) (,y . ,z))

a substitution?

22 Not here,
since we forbid a substitution from containing associations that create a cycle: if x, y, and z are already fused, and x is fresh in the substitution, adding the association `(,x . ,y) would have created a cycle.

Is

`((,x . (a ,y)) (,z . ,w) (,y . (,x)))

a substitution?

23 Not here,

since we forbid a substitution from containing associations that create a cycle: x is the same as `(a ,y), and $y$ is the same as `(,x). Therefore `(a (,x)) is the same as $x$, a variable occurring in `(a (,x)).

What is the value of

(*occurs?* x x '())

24 #t,

To begin with, *occurs?*'s second argument, the variable x, is *walk*'d. The **let** is used to hold the value of that *walk*, and since the substitution is empty, we know that every variable must be fresh. So in the definition of *occurs?*, (*var?* v), where v is x is #t, and thus the first argument, also x, is the same as v.

What is the value of

(*occurs?* x `(,y) `((,y . ,x)))

25 #t,

since *occurs?* walks recursively over the *cars* and *cdrs* of `(,y).

What is the value of

(*ext-s* x `(,x) *empty-s*)

26 #f,

since we do *not* permit associations between a variable and a value in which that variable occurs (see frame 23).

What is the value of

(*ext-s* x `(,y) `((,y . ,x)))

27 #f,

since we do *not* permit associations between a variable and a value in which that variable occurs (see frame 23).

What is the value of

```
(let ((s `((,z . ,x) (,y . ,z))))
  (let ((s (ext-s x 'e s)))
    (and s (walk y s))))
```

28 e,

We are asking what is the value of *walk*ing *y* after *cons*ing the association `(,x . e) onto that substitution.

---

walk and *ext-s* are used in *unify*.†

```
(define (unify u v s)
  (let ((u (walk u s)) (v (walk v s)))
    (cond
      ((eqv? u v) s)
      ((var? u) (ext-s u v s))
      ((var? v) (ext-s v u s))
      ((and (pair? u) (pair? v))
       (let ((s (unify (car u) (car v) s)))
         (and s
           (unify (cdr u) (cdr v) s))))
      (else #f))))
```

What kinds of values are produced by *unify*

† Thank you Jacques Herbrand (1908–1931) and John Alan Robinson (1930–2016), and thanks Dag Prawitz (1936–).

29 Either #f or the substitution *s* extended with zero or more associations, where the cycle conditions in frames 22 and 23 can lead to #f.

What is the first thing that happens in *unify*

30 We use **let**, which binds *u* and *v* to their *walk*'d values. If *u* *walk*s to a variable, then *u* is fresh, and likewise if *v* *walk*s to a variable, then *v* is fresh.

What is the purpose of the *eqv?* test in *unify*'s first **cond** line?

31 If *u* and *v* are the same according to *eqv?*, we do not extend the substitution. *eqv?* works for strings, characters, numbers, Booleans, symbols, (), and our variables.

Describe *unify*'s second **cond** line.	32	If (*var? u*) is #t, then *u* is fresh, and therefore *u* is the first argument when attempting to extend *s*.
And describe *unify*'s third **cond** line.	33	If (*var? v*) is #t, then *v* is fresh, and therefore *v* is the first argument when attempting to extend *s*.
What happens on *unify*'s fourth **cond** line, when both *u* and *v* are pairs?	34	We attempt to unify the *car* of *u* with the *car* of *v*. If they unify, we get a substitution, which we use to attempt to unify the *cdr* of *u* with the *cdr* of *v*.
This completes the definition of *unify*.	35	Okay.

⟹ Take a break after the 1st course! ⟸

Pumpkin soup.

—or—

Tomato salad with fresh basil and avocado slices.

—or—

A platter of little lentil cakes with hot powder (idli-milagai-podi).

Welcome back.	36	Can we now discuss ≡?
Not yet. We need one more idea: *streams*.	37	What is a stream?

A stream is either the empty list, a pair whose *cdr* is a stream, or a *suspension.*

38 What is a suspension?

A suspension is a function formed from (**lambda** () *body*) where ((**lambda** () *body*)) is a stream.

39 Okay.

Here's a stream of symbols,

```
(cons 'a
  (cons 'b
    (cons 'c
      (cons 'd '()))))).
```

40 Isn't that just a proper list?

Yes. Here is another stream of symbols,

```
(cons 'a
  (cons 'b
    (lambda ()
      (cons 'c
        (cons 'd '())))))).
```

What type of stream is the second argument to the second *cons*

41 The **lambda** expression,

```
(lambda ()
  (cons 'c
    (cons 'd '()))),
```

is a suspension.

And here is one more stream,

```
(lambda ()
  (cons 'a
    (cons 'b
      (cons 'c
        (cons 'd '())))))).
```

Why is the expression a stream?

42 The **lambda** expression is a stream, because it is a **lambda** expression of the form (**lambda** () . . .) and we already know that this *cons* expression is a stream, since it is the list from frame 40.

Here is ≡.

```
(define (≡ u v)
  (lambda (s)
    (let ((s (unify u v s)))
      (if s `(,s) '()))))
```

43 What does ≡ produce?

It produces a *goal*. Here are two more goals.

```
(define #s
  (lambda (s)
    `(,s)))

(define #u
  (lambda (s)
    '()))
```

44 What is a goal?

Each of ≡, #s, and #u has a

```
(lambda (s)
  ...).
```

A goal is a function that expects a substitution and, if it returns, produces a stream of substitutions.

45 Thus, *s* is a substitution. And every goal produces a stream of substitutions.

From now on, all our streams are streams of substitutions and we use "*stream*" to mean "*stream of substitutions.*"

46 Okay.

Look at the definitions of the goals #s, #u, and (≡ *u* *v*). What sizes are the streams these goals produce?

47 #s produces singleton streams and #u produces the empty stream, while goals like (≡ *u* *v*) can produce either singleton streams or the empty stream.

May we try out these streams?

Let's. Here is an example. What is the value of

((≡ #t #f) *empty-s*)

48 ().

Because #t and #f do not unify in the empty substitution, or indeed in any substitution, the goal produces the empty stream.

Is there a simpler way to write

((≡ #t #f) *empty-s*)

49 ((≡ #t #f) *empty-s*) is the same as

(#u *empty-s*).

And is there a simpler way to write

((≡ #f #f) *empty-s*)

50 How about

(#s *empty-s*)?

What is the value of

((≡ x y) *empty-s*)

51 `(((,$x$ . ,$y$))), a singleton of the substitution `((,x . ,y)),† since unifying x and y extends this substitution with an association of y to x.

† The value of ((≡ y x) *empty-s*) is instead a singleton of the substitution `((,y . ,x)). To ensure **The First Law of ≡**, we *reify* each value (see frame 104).

⟹ Take a break after the 2nd course! ⟸

Spinach salad.

—or—

Roasted fingerling potatoes.

—or—

A moong daal, cucumber, and carrot salad (kosambari).

When do we need **cond**^{e}

52 Never. As we have seen in frame 1:88, we can always replace a **cond**^{e} with uses of $disj_2$ and $conj_2$.

Recall ($disj_2$ ($\equiv$ 'olive x) ($\equiv$ 'oil x)) from frame 1:58.

What is the value of

(($disj_2$ ($\equiv$ 'olive x) ($\equiv$ 'oil x)) *empty-s*)

53 \`(((,x . olive)) ((,x . oil))),

a stream of size two. The first associates olive with x, and the second associates oil with x.

Here is $disj_2$.

```
(define (disj₂ g₁ g₂)
  (lambda (s)
    (append∞ (g₁ s) (g₂ s))))
```

What are g_1 and g_2?

54 Are g_1 and g_2 goals?

Exactly. Does $disj_2$ produce a goal?

55 It produces a function that expects a substitution as an argument. Therefore, if $append^\infty$ produces a stream, then $disj_2$ produces a goal.

Here is $append^\infty$.

```
(define (append∞ s∞ t∞)
  (cond
    ((null? s∞) t∞)
    ((pair? s∞)
     (cons (car s∞)
       (append∞ (cdr s∞) t∞)))
    (else (lambda ()
            (append∞ t∞ (s∞))))))
```

What are s^∞ and t^∞

56 Each must be a stream.

Yes. What might we name *append*$^\infty$, if its third **cond** line were absent?

57 It would then behave the same as *append* in frame 4:1.

What type of stream is s^∞ in the answer of *append*$^\infty$'s third **cond** line?

58 In the third **cond** line, s^∞ must be a suspension.

What type of stream is

```
(lambda ()
  (append∞ t∞ (s∞)))
```

in the answer of *append*$^\infty$'s third **cond** line?

59 In the third **cond** line,

```
(lambda ()
  (append∞ t∞ (s∞)))
```

is also a suspension.

Look carefully at the suspension in *append*$^\infty$. The suspension's body,

```
(append∞ t∞ (s∞)),
```

swaps the arguments to *append*$^\infty$, and (s^∞) *forces* the suspension s^∞.

When is the suspension s^∞ forced?

60 The suspension s^∞ is forced when the suspension

```
(lambda ()
  (append∞ t∞ (s∞)))
```

is itself forced.

Here is the relation *never*^{o} from frame 6:14 with **define** instead of **defrel**,

```
(define (nevero)
  (lambda (s)
    (lambda ()
      ((nevero) s)))).
```

61 Does *never*^{o} produce a goal?

Yes it does. What is the value of

```
((nevero) empty-s)
```

62 A suspension.
never^o is a relation that, when invoked, produces a goal. The goal, when given a substitution, here *empty-s*, produces a suspension in the same way as (*never*^{o}), and so on.

What is the value of

```
(let ((s∞ ((disj₂
             (≡ 'olive x)
             (neverᵒ))
           empty-s)))
  s∞)
```

63 This stream, s^∞, is a pair whose *car* is the substitution `((,x . olive)) and whose *cdr* is a stream.

What is the value of

```
(let ((s∞ ((disj₂
             (neverᵒ)
             (≡ 'olive x))
           empty-s)))
  s∞)
```

where the two expressions in $disj_2$ have been swapped?

64 This stream, s^∞, is a suspension.

Why isn't the value a pair whose *car* is the substitution `((,x . olive)) and whose *cdr* is a suspension, as in frame 63?

65 Because $disj_2$ uses $append^\infty$, and the answer of the third **cond** line of $append^\infty$ is a suspension.

How do we get the substitution `((,x . olive)) out of that suspension?

By forcing the suspension s^∞.

What is the value of

```
(let ((s∞ ((disj₂
             (neverᵒ)
             (≡ 'olive x))
           empty-s)))
  (s∞))
```

66 A pair whose *car* is the substitution `((,x . olive)) and whose *cdr* is a stream like the value in frame 63.

Describe how $append^\infty$ merges the streams

((≡ 'olive x) *empty-s*)

and

((*never*^{o}) *empty-s*)

so that we can see the substitution

`((,x . olive)).

67 As described in frame 60, each time we force a suspension produced by the third **cond** line of $append^\infty$, we swap the arguments to $append^\infty$ as the answer of that **cond** line. When we force the suspension, what was the second argument, t^∞, becomes the first argument. Thus, the second argument to $disj_2$, the productive stream, ((≡ 'olive x) *empty-s*), becomes the first argument to $append^\infty$ of the recursion in the third **cond** line.

When does the recursion in $append^\infty$'s third **cond** line merge these streams?

68 If the result of the third **cond** line is forced, then $append^\infty$'s recursion merges these streams. And because of this, ((≡ 'olive x) *empty-s*) produces a value.

Here is the relation *always*^{o} from frame 6:1 with **define** instead of **defrel**,

```
(define (alwayso)
  (lambda (s)
    (lambda ()
      ((disj2 #s (alwayso)) s)))).
```

What is the value of

(((*always*^{o}) *empty-s*))

69 A pair whose *car* is (), the empty substitution, and whose *cdr* is a stream.

Using *always*^{o}, how would we create a list of the first empty substitution?

70 Like this,

```
(let ((s∞ (((alwayso) empty-s))))
  (cons (car s∞) '())).
```

We can only use the *car* of a stream if that stream is a pair.

How would we create a list of the first two empty substitutions?

71 That would be tedious,

```
(let ((s∞ (((alwaysᵒ) empty-s))))
  (cons (car s∞)
    (let ((s∞ ((cdr s∞))))
      (cons (car s∞) '()))))).
```

Here, ((*always*^{o}) *empty-s*) is a suspension. Forcing the suspension produces a pair. The *car* of the pair is a substitution. The *cdr* of the pair is a new suspension. Forcing the new suspension produces yet another pair.

How would we create a list of the first three empty substitutions?

72 That would be more tedious,

```
(let ((s∞ (((alwaysᵒ) empty-s))))
  (cons (car s∞)
    (let ((s∞ ((cdr s∞))))
      (cons (car s∞)
        (let ((s∞ ((cdr s∞))))
          (cons (car s∞) '())))))))).
```

How would we create a list of the first thirty-seven empty substitutions?

73 That would be most tedious.

Can we keep track of how many substitutions we still need?

Need a break?

Take Five

Thank you, Dave Brubeck (1920–2012).

Yes, using $take^\infty$.

```
(define (take∞ n s∞)
  (cond
    ((and n (zero? n)) '())
    ((null? s∞) '())
    ((pair? s∞)
     (cons (car s∞)
       (take∞ (and n (sub1 n))
         (cdr s∞))))
    (else (take∞ n (s∞)))))
```

Describe what $take^\infty$ does when n is a number.

74 When given a number n and a stream s^∞, if $take^\infty$ returns, it produces a list of at most n values. When n is a number, the expression (**and** n e) behaves the same as the expression e.

Yes. What is the value of

($take^\infty$ 1 (($never^o$) *empty-s*))

75 It has no value.

The value of (($never^o$) *empty-s*) is a suspension. Every suspension created by $never^o$, when forced, creates another similar suspension. Thus every use of $take^\infty$ causes another use of $take^\infty$.

How does $take^\infty$ differ when n is `#f`

76 When n is `#f`, the expression (**and** n e) behaves the same as `#f`. Thus, the recursion in $take^\infty$'s last **cond** line behaves the same as

($take^\infty$ `#f` (s^∞)).

Furthermore, when n is `#f`, the first **cond** question is never true. Thus if $take^\infty$ returns, it produces a list of *all* the values.

Yes. Use $take^\infty$ and $always^o$ to make a list of three empty substitutions.

77 It must be this,

($take^\infty$ 3 (($always^o$) *empty-s*))

has the value (() () ()).

What is the value of

```
(take∞ #f ((alwaysº) empty-s))
```

78 It has no value, because the stream produced by ((*always*^{o}) *empty-s*) can always produce another substitution for *take*$^\infty$.

What is the value of

```
(let ((k (length
           (take∞ 5
             ((disj₂ (≡ 'olive x) (≡ 'oil x))
              empty-s)))))
  `(Found ,k not 5 substitutions))
```

79 (Found 2 not 5 substitutions).

And what is the value of

```
(map† length
  (take∞ 5
    ((disj₂ (≡ 'olive x) (≡ 'oil x))
     empty-s)))
```

80 (1 1), since each substitution has one association.

† *map* takes a function f and a list *ls* and builds a list (using *cons*), where each element of that list is produced by applying f to the corresponding element of *ls*.

⟹ Take a break after the 3rd course! ⟸

Roasted brussel sprouts.

—or—

Peppers stuffed with lentils and buckwheat groats.

—or—

Rice with tamarind sauce and vegetables (bisi-bele-bath).

Here is $conj_2$.

```
(define (conj₂ g₁ g₂)
  (lambda (s)
    (append-map∞ g₂ (g₁ s))))
```

What are g_1 and g_2?

81 Are g_1 and g_2 goals, again?

Yes. Does $conj_2$ produce a goal?

82 Probably,
since there's a (**lambda** (s) ...). So we presume *append-map*$^\infty$ produces a stream.

What is (g_1 s)?

83 It must be a stream.

Yes. Here is the definition of *append-map*$^\infty$.†

```
(define (append-map∞ g s∞)
  (cond
    ((null? s∞) '())
    ((pair? s∞)
     (append∞ (g (car s∞))
       (append-map∞ g (cdr s∞))))
    (else (lambda ()
            (append-map∞ g (s∞))))))
```

† If *append-map*$^\infty$'s third **cond** line and *append*$^\infty$'s third **cond** line were absent, *append-map*$^\infty$ would then behave the same as *append-map*. *append-map* is like *map* (see frame 80), but it uses *append* instead of *cons* to build its result.

84 How does it work?

If s^∞ were (()), which **cond** line would be used?

85 The second **cond** line.

What would be the value of (*car* s^∞) | 86 The empty substitution ().

If *g* were a goal, what would (*g* (*car* s^∞)) be when s^∞ is a pair? | 87 (*g* (*car* s^∞)) would be a stream.

And we did presume that *append-map*$^\infty$ would produce a stream. | 88 Indeed, we did.

What would *append*$^\infty$ produce, given two streams as arguments? | 89 A stream. Therefore, *conj*$_2$ would indeed produce a goal.

⟹ Take a break after the 4th course! ⟸

Linguini pasta in cashew cream sauce.

—or—

Thinly-sliced fennel with lemon juice and fresh thyme.

—or—

Rice with curds, pomegranate seeds, ginger, and chili (thayir-sadam)**.**

We define the function *call/fresh* to introduce variables.

```
(define (call/fresh name f)
  (f (var name)))
```

Although *name* is used, it is ignored.

90 What does *call/fresh* expect as its second argument?

91 *call/fresh* expects its second argument to be a lambda expression. More specifically, that lambda expression should expect a variable and produce a goal. That goal then has access to the variable just created. Give an example of such an *f*.

Something like

```
(lambda (fruit)
  (≡ 'plum fruit)),
```

which then could be passed a variable,

```
(take∞ 1
  ((call/fresh 'kiwi
     (lambda (fruit)
       (≡ 'plum fruit)))
   empty-s)).
```

---

92 When would it make sense to use distinct symbols for variables?

When we *present* values.

---

93 Yes. Every variable that we present is presented as a corresponding symbol: an underscore followed by a natural number. We call these symbols *reified variables* as in frame 1:17.

How can we create a reified variable given a number?

How about this[†]?

```
(define (reify-name n)
  (string→symbol
    (string-append "_"
      (number→string n))))
```

† Avoid using constants that resemble reified variables, since this could cause confusion.

---

94 Now that we can create reified variables, how do we associate reified variables with variables?

Wouldn't the association of variables with reified variables just be another kind of substitution?

---

95 Yes, we call such a substitution a *reified-name* substitution. What is the reified-name substitution for the fresh variables in the value `(,x ,y ,x ,z ,z)

`((,z . $_2$) (,y . $_1$) (,x . $_0$)).

What is the reified value of `(,x ,y ,x ,z ,z), using the reified-name substitution from the previous frame?

96 ($_0$ $_1$ $_0$ $_2$ $_2$).

Recall the *walk* expression from frame 17

```
(walk w
  `((,x . b) (,z . ,y) (,w . (,x e ,z))))
```

has the value `(,x e ,z).

What is the value of

```
(walk* w
  `((,x . b) (,z . ,y) (,w . (,x e ,z))))
```

97 The list `(b e ,y).
First, *walk** *walk*s w to `(,$x$ e ,$z$). *walk*\* then recursively *walk*\*s $x$ and `(e ,z).

Here is *walk**.

```
(define (walk* v s)
  (let ((v (walk v s)))
    (cond
      ((var? v) v)
      ((pair? v)
       (cons
         (walk* (car v) s)
         (walk* (cdr v) s)))
      (else v))))
```

Is *walk** recursive?

98 Yes, and it's also useful.[†]

[†] Here is **project** (pronounced "pro·ject").

```
(define-syntax project
  (syntax-rules ()
    ((project (x ...) g ...)
     (lambda (s)
       (let ((x (walk* x s)) ...)
         ((conj g ...) s))))))
```

project behaves like **fresh**, but it binds different values to the lexical variables. **project** binds *walk**'d values, whereas **fresh** binds variables using *var*.

When do the values of (*walk** v s) and (*walk* v s) differ?

99 They differ when v *walk*s in s to a pair, and the pair contains a variable that has an association in s.

Does *walk**'s behavior differ from *walk*'s behavior if v, the result of *walk*, is a variable?

100 No.

101 How does *walk**'s behavior differ from *walk*'s behavior if *v*, the result of *walk*, is a pair?

If *v*'s *walk*'d value is a pair, the second **cond** line of *walk** is used. Then, *walk** constructs a new pair of the *walk**'d values in that pair, whereas the *walk*'d value is just *v*.

---

102 If *v*'s *walk*'d value is neither a variable nor a pair, does *walk** behave like *walk*

Yes.

---

103 What property holds when a value is *walk**'d?

If a value is *walk**'d in a substitution *s*, and *walk** produces a value *v*, then we know that each variable in *v* is fresh.

---

104 Here is *reify-s*, which initially expects a value *v* and an empty reified-name substitution *r*.

```
(define (reify-s v r)
  (let ((v (walk v r)))
    (cond
      ((var? v)
       (let ((n (length r)))
         (let ((rn (reify-name n)))
           (cons `(,v . ,rn) r))))
      ((pair? v)
       (let ((r (reify-s (car v) r)))
         (reify-s (cdr v) r)))
      (else r))))
```

What definition is *reify-s* reminiscent of?

unify.

reify-s, unlike *unify*, expects only one value in addition to a substitution. Also, *reify-s* cannot produce #f. But, like *unify*, *reify-s* begins by *walk*ing *v*. Then in both cases, if the *walk*'d *v* is a variable, we know it is fresh and we use that fresh variable to extend the substitution. Unlike in *unify*, no *occurs?* is needed in *reify-s*. In both cases, if *v* is a pair, we first produce a new substitution based on the *car* of the pair. That substitution can then be extended using the *cdr* of the pair. And, there is a case where the substitution remains unchanged.

---

105 Right. What is the first thing that happens in *reify-s*

We use **let**, which gives a *walk*'d (and possibly different) value to *v*.

Describe *reify-s*'s first **cond** line.

106 If (*var? v*) is #t, then *v* is a fresh variable in *r*, and therefore can be used in extending *r* with a reified variable.

Why is *length* used?

107 Every time *reify-s* extends *r*, *length* produces a unique number to pass to *reify-name*.

Describe *reify-s*'s second **cond** line, when *v* is a pair.

108 We extend the reified-name substitution with *v*'s *car*, and extend *that* substitution to make another reified-name substitution with *v*'s *cdr*.

When *v* is neither a variable nor a pair, what is the result?

109 It is the current reified-name substitution.

Now that we know how to create a reified-name substitution, how should we use the substitution to replace all the fresh variables in a value?

110 We use *walk** in the reified-name substitution to replace all the variables in the value.

Consider the definition of *reify*, which relies on *reify-s*.

```
(define (reify v)
  (lambda (s)
    (let ((v (walk* v s)))
      (let ((r (reify-s v empty-s)))
        (walk* v r)))))
```

Is *reify* recursive?

111 No, *reify* is not recursive.

Describe the behavior of the expression (*walk* v r*) in *reify*'s last line.

112 Each fresh variable in *v* is replaced by its reified variable in the reified-name substitution *r*.

What is the value of

```
(let ((a1 `(,x . (,u ,w ,y ,z ((ice) ,z))))
      (a2 `(,y . corn))
      (a3 `(,w . (,v ,u))))
  (let ((s `(,a1 ,a2 ,a3)))
    ((reify x) s)))
```

113 (_0 (_1 _0) corn _2 ((ice) _2)).

What is the value of

```
(map (reify x)
  (take∞ 5
    ((disj2 (≡ 'olive x) (≡ 'oil x))
     empty-s)))
```

114 (olive oil).

We can combine *take*$^{\infty}$ with passing the empty substitution to a goal.

```
(define (run-goal n g)
  (take∞ n (g empty-s)))
```

Using *run-goal*, rewrite the expression in the previous frame.

115 Here it is,

```
(map (reify x)
  (run-goal 5
    (disj2 (≡ 'olive x) (≡ 'oil x)))).
```

Let's put the pieces together!

We can now define *append*^{o} from frame 4:41, replacing **cond**^{e}, **fresh**, and **defrel** with the functions defined in this chapter.

116 Like this,

```
(define (appendᵒ l t out)
  (lambda (s)
    (lambda ()
      ((disj₂
         (conj₂ (nullᵒ l) (≡ t out))
         (call/fresh 'a
           (lambda (a)
             (call/fresh 'd
               (lambda (d)
                 (call/fresh 'res
                   (lambda (res)
                     (conj₂
                       (consᵒ a d l)
                       (conj₂
                         (consᵒ a res out)
                         (appendᵒ d t
                           res))))))))))
       s))))).
```

Now, the argument to *run-goal* is #f instead of a number, so that we get *all* the values,

```
(let ((q (var 'q)))
  (map (reify q)
    (run-goal #f
      (call/fresh 'x
        (lambda (x)
          (call/fresh 'y
            (lambda (y)
              (conj₂
                (≡ `(,x ,y) q)
                (appendᵒ x y
                  '(cake & ice d t)))))))))).
```

117 And behold, we get the result in frame 4:42,

```
((() (cake & ice d t))
 ((cake) (& ice d t))
 ((cake &) (ice d t))
 ((cake & ice) (d t))
 ((cake & ice d) (t))
 ((cake & ice d t) ())).
```

These last few frames should aid understanding the hygienic† rewrite macros on page 177: **defrel**, **run**, **run***, **fresh**, and **cond**^{e}.

118 Not only is the result the same, but the **run*** expression in frame 4:42 rewrites to the *run-goal* expression in the previous frame. And the *append*^{o} definition in frame 4:41 is virtually the same *append*^{o} definition in frame 116.

† Thanks, Eugene Kohlbecker (1954–).

⟹ Take a break after the 5th course! ⟸

Lemon sorbet.

—or—

Espresso.

—or—

Jackfruit dessert with a dollop of coconut cream (chakka-pradhaman).

In all the excitement, have we forgotten something?

119 What about **cond**^{a} and **cond**^{u}?

cond^a relies on *ifte*, so let's start there.

120 Okay.

What is the value of

```
((ifte #s
   (≡ #f y)
   (≡ #t y))
 empty-s)
```

121 `(((,y . #f))),
because the first goal #s succeeds, so we try the second goal (≡ #f *y*).

What is the value of

```
((ifte #u
   (≡ #f y)
   (≡ #t y))
 empty-s)
```

122 `(((,y . #t))),
because the first goal #u fails, so we instead try the third goal (≡ #t y).

What is the value of

```
((ifte (≡ #t x)
   (≡ #f y)
   (≡ #t y))
 empty-s)
```

123 `(((,y . #f) (,x . #t))),
because the first goal (≡ #t x) succeeds, producing a stream of one substitution, so we try the second goal on that substitution.

What is the value of

```
((ifte (disj₂ (≡ #t x) (≡ #f x))
   (≡ #f y)
   (≡ #t y))
 empty-s)
```

124 `(((,y . #f) (,x . #t)) ((,y . #f) (,x . #f))),
because the first goal ($disj_2$ (≡ #t x) (≡ #f x)) succeeds, producing a stream of two substitutions, so we try the second goal on *each* of those substitutions.

What might the name *ifte*† suggest?

125 **if**-**t**hen-**e**lse.

† Here is the expression in frame 124 using **cond**^{a} rather than *ifte*.

```
((condᵃ
   ((disj₂ (≡ #t x) (≡ #f x)) (≡ #f y))
   ((≡ #t y)))
 empty-s)
```

This use of **cond**^{a}, however, violates **The Second Commandment** as in frames 9:11 and 12. Although **The Second Commandment** is described in terms of **cond**^{a}, the uses of *ifte* in frames 123 and 124 violate the spirit of this commandment.

Here is *ifte*.

```
(define (ifte g1 g2 g3)
  (lambda (s)
    (let loop ((s∞ (g1 s)))
      (cond
        ((null? s∞) (g3 s))
        ((pair? s∞)
         (append-map∞ g2 s∞))
        (else (lambda ()
                (loop (s∞))))))))
```

Is *ifte* recursive?

126 No, but *ifte*'s helper, *loop*, is recursive.

What does *ifte* produce?

127 A goal.

The body of that goal is

(**let** *loop* ((s^∞ (g_1 s))) ...).

What does **let** *loop*'s (**cond** ...) produce?

128 The (**cond** ...) produces a stream.

Where have we seen these same **cond** questions?

129 In the definitions of *append*$^\infty$ and *append-map*$^\infty$, and in the last three lines in the definition of *take*$^\infty$.

What is the value of

```
((ifte (once (disj₂ (≡ #t x) (≡ #f x)))†
   (≡ #f y)
   (≡ #t y))
 empty-s)
```

130 `(((,y . #f) (,x . #t))), because the first goal ($disj_2$ (≡ #t x) (≡ #f x)) succeeds *once*, producing a stream of a single substitution, so we try the second goal on that substitution.

† Although **The Second Commandment** is described in terms of **cond**^{a} and **cond**^{u}, these expand into expressions that use *ifte* and *once* (appendix A). The expression in this frame is equivalent to a **cond**^{u} expression that violates **The Second Commandment** as in frame 9:19.

Here is *once*.

```
(define (once g)
  (lambda (s)
    (let loop ((s∞ (g s)))
      (cond
        ((null? s∞) '())
        ((pair? s∞)
         (cons (car s∞) '()))
        (else (lambda ()
                (loop (s∞))))))))
```

What is the value when s^∞ is a pair?

131 The value is a singleton stream.

In *once*, what happens to the remaining substitutions in s^∞

132 They vanish!

The end, sort of.

Time for vacation.

Are you back yet?

Get ready to connect the wires!

Connecting the Wires

In chapter 10 we define functions for a low-level relational programming language. We now define—and explain how to read—*macros*, which extend Scheme's syntax to provide the language used in most of the book. We could instead interpret our programs as data, as in the Scheme interpreter in chapter 10 of *The Little Schemer*.

Recall $disj_2$ from frame 10:54.

Here is a simple $disj_2$ expression:

($disj_2$ (≡ 'tea 'tea) #u).

We now add the syntax (**disj** *g* ...).

(**disj** (≡ 'tea 'tea) #u #s)

macro expands to the expression

($disj_2$ (≡ 'tea 'tea) ($disj_2$ #u #s)),

which does not contain **disj**. Here are the helper macros **disj** and **conj**.

```
(define-syntax disj
  (syntax-rules ()
    ((disj) #u)
    ((disj g) g)
    ((disj g0 g ...) (disj2 g0 (disj g ...)))))
(define-syntax conj
  (syntax-rules ()
    ((conj) #s)
    ((conj g) g)
    ((conj g0 g ...) (conj2 g0 (conj g ...)))))
```

syntax-rules begins with a keyword list, empty here, followed by one or more rules. Each rule has a left and right side. The first rule says that (**disj**) expands to #u. The second rule says that (**disj** *g*) expands to *g*. In the last rule "g_0 *g* ..." means at least one goal expression, since "*g* ..." means zero or more goal expressions. The right-hand side expands to a $disj_2$ of two goal expressions: g_0, and a **disj** macro expansion with one fewer goal expressions. **conj** behaves like **disj** with $disj_2$ replaced by $conj_2$ and #u replaced by #s.

Each **defrel** expression defines a new function. **run**'s first rule and **fresh**'s second rule scope each variable "x_0 *x* ..." within "*g* ...". **run**'s second rule scopes *q* within "*g* ...". The second "..." indicates each **cond**^{e} expression may have zero lines. **cond**^{u} expands to a **cond**^{a}.

```
(define-syntax defrel
  (syntax-rules ()
    ((defrel (name x ...) g ...)
     (define (name x ...)
       (lambda (s)
         (lambda ()
           ((conj g ...) s)))))))
```

```
(define-syntax run
  (syntax-rules ()
    ((run n (x0 x ...) g ...)
     (run n q (fresh (x0 x ...)
                (≡ `(,x0 ,x ...) q) g ...)))
    ((run n q g ...)
     (let ((q (var 'q)))
       (map (reify q)
         (run-goal n (conj g ...)))))))

(define-syntax run*
  (syntax-rules ()
    ((run* q g ...) (run #f q g ...))))
```

```
(define-syntax fresh
  (syntax-rules ()
    ((fresh () g ...) (conj g ...))
    ((fresh (x0 x ...) g ...)
     (call/fresh 'x0
       (lambda (x0)
         (fresh (x ...) g ...))))))

(define-syntax conde
  (syntax-rules ()
    ((conde (g ...) ...)
     (disj (conj g ...) ...))))
```

```
(define-syntax conda
  (syntax-rules ()
    ((conda (g0 g ...)) (conj g0 g ...))
    ((conda (g0 g ...) ln ...)
     (ifte g0 (conj g ...) (conda ln ...)))))

(define-syntax condu
  (syntax-rules ()
    ((condu (g0 g ...) ...)
     (conda ((once g0) g ...) ...))))
```

Welcome to the Club

Here is a small collection of entertaining and illuminating books.

Carroll, Lewis. *The Annotated Alice: The Definitive Edition.* W. W. Norton & Company, New York, 1999. Introduction and notes by Martin Gardner.

Franzén, Torkel. *Gödel's Theorem: An Incomplete Guide to Its Use and Abuse.* A. K. Peters Ltd., Wellesley, MA, 2005.

Hein, Piet. *Grooks.* The MIT Press, 1960.

Hofstadter, Douglas R. *Gödel, Escher, Bach: An Eternal Golden Braid.* Basic Books, Inc., 1979.

Nagel, Ernest, and James R. Newman. *Gödel's Proof.* New York University Press, 1958.

Smullyan, Raymond. *To Mock a Mockingbird.* Alfred A. Knopf, Inc., 1985.

Suppes, Patrick. *Introduction to Logic.* Van Nostrand Co., 1957.

Afterword

It is commonplace to note that computer technology affects almost all aspects of our lives today, from the way we do our banking, to the games we play and to the way we interact with our friends. Because of its all-pervasive nature, the more we understand how it works and the better we understand how to control it, the better we will be able to survive and prosper in the future.

The importance of improving our understanding of computer technology has been recognised by the educational community, with the result that computing is rapidly becoming a core academic subject in primary and secondary schools. Unfortunately, few school teachers have the background and the training needed to deal with this challenge, which is made worse by the confusing variety of computer languages and computing paradigms that are competing for adoption.

Even more challenging for teachers in many respects is the promotion of computational thinking as a basic problem solving skill that applies not only to computing but to virtually all problem domains. Teachers have to decide not only what computer languages to teach, but whether to teach children to think imperatively, declaratively, object-orientedly, or in one of the many other ways in which computers are programmed today.

Computer scientists by and large have not been very helpful in dealing with this state of confusion. The subject of computing has become so vast that few computer scientists are able or willing to venture outside the confines of their own specialised sub-disciplines, with the consequence that the gap between different approaches to computing seems to be widening rather than narrowing. Instead of serving as a true science, concerned with unifying different approaches and different paradigms, computer science has all too often been magnifying the differences and shying away from the big issues.

This is where *The Reasoned Schemer* makes an important contribution, showing how to bridge the gap between functional programming and relational (or logic) programming—not combining the two in one heterogeneous, hybrid system, but showing how the two are deeply related. Moreover, it doesn't rest content with merely addressing the experts, but it aims to educate the next generation of laypeople and experts, for a day when Computer Science will genuinely be worthy of its title. And, because computing is not disjoint from other academic disciplines, it also builds upon and strengthens the links between mathematics and computing.

The Reasoned Schemer is not just a book for the future, showing the way to build bridges between different paradigms. But it is also a book that honours the past in its use of the Socratic method to engage the reader. It is a book for all time, and a book that deserves to serve as an example to others.

Robert A. Kowalski
Petworth, West Sussex, England
August 2017

Index

fresh
defrel
#s
conde
conda
#u
condu
run*
λ
reify
disj2
conj2
unify
run-goal
≡
run

Index

Italic page numbers refer to definitions.